TEN PLE

You've Never Met Are About To

CHANGE YOUR
Life

Sam Rowland

TEN PEOPLE YOU'VE NEVER MET
Are About to Change Your Life

Unless otherwise indicated, Scripture quotations are taken from the Holy Bible, New International Version®. Copyright © 1973, 1978, 1984 International Bible Society. Used by permission of Zondervan. All rights reserved.

Scripture quotations marked NLT are taken from the Holy Bible, New Living Translation. Copyright © 1996. Used by permission of Tyndale House Publishers, Inc., Wheaton, Illinois 60189. All rights reserved. Scripture quotations marked MSG from The Message. Copyright © 1993, 1994, 1995, 1996, 2000, 2001, 2002. Used by permission of NavPress Publishing Group.

ISBN-10: 1-926676-36-X
ISBN-13: 978-1-926676-36-4

Printed in Canada.

Printed by Word Alive Press
131 Cordite Road, Winnipeg, MB R3W 1S1
www.wordalivepress.ca

WORD ALIVE PRESS
Just Write!

To the person who has impacted my life more profoundly than anyone else: my wife Rita.

ACKNOWLEDGEMENTS

Special thanks to Ken Pudlas, Roy Salmond, Brian Brown, Andy Harrington, Jordan Bateman, John Rissling, Paul Craig, Bill Hogg, James Rowland, Dale Lutz, Karl & Wendy Janzen, Jos and Sylvia Holtzhausen, Don and Vel Kinnie, Evan Braun, Stuart Dahl, Ant Snyman, and Peter and Elsje Hannah.

TABLE OF CONTENTS

INTRODUCTION

Ten people you've never met are about to change your life. I know this because they changed mine, in spite of my best efforts to remain unchanged. For a long time, I resisted the idea of writing this book. In the end, though, I realized that I couldn't keep these people, and the gifts they had given, to myself.

Every one of these ten people is real flesh and blood. They are not fictional. They are not "composites" of several interesting characters that have been pooled into one really inspirational soul.

None of these accounts are simply "based" on a true story either; each one is a true story in itself. I have met and personally interacted with each person that you will encounter in this book, with the exception of one (you'll understand why when the time is right).

One page at a time, I will unpack the bittersweet beauty of their stories for you. I'll share a little bit of my story, too. But the soundtrack to all of this will be your story, and that will make your reading of this book unique.

At ten pivotal points in my journey, these ten people's lives have intersected with my life. Now, they will intersect with yours.

SAM ROWLAND
July 2009

CHAPTER ONE

STILL STANDING... STILL STANDING
(Ten Minutes with Kandume Will Change You)

I was on one of my very first trips to Africa when I met him, and finding him was like winning a lottery that I had not bought a ticket for: totally unexpected, a complete gift. And not just any kind of lottery either, but one of those lotteries that keeps paying month after month, and year after year, for the rest of your life. His name was Kandume (kan-doo-may), and his heart was even bigger than his huge gap-toothed smile.

After a long night and day of driving north through the African desert towards Angola, we had finally arrived at Kandume's home on the outskirts of Oshakati, Namibia. This simple cement-block house was to be our headquarters for two weeks as we gave presentations on AIDS awareness and life skills at schools, prisons, and churches in the area.

I got out of the truck after the long drive, stood and stretched my tired body, weary from the heat—42 degrees Celsius (108 degrees Fahrenheit) in the shade.

Within seconds, Kandume bounded out the door towards our rag tag team, exuding a warmth that outshone the hot African sun. His electric smile and bear-pawed handshake morphed into a hug and, at that moment, I felt like the most important person in the world. So warm was his welcome that had I not been a blue-eyed white man from Canada, I would have sworn that he had mistaken me for his own long-lost son!

As he spoke, his conversation was full of life and light, but his hoarse voice and bare, twisted, awkward feet made it clear that his had been a hard life. His voice and body had paid a price because of his particular journey.

Over the next few days, we spent time with him and "Momma Kandume" over meals, through times of prayer, and during long conversations about everything from geography to politics to people.

I heard him preach at the little Baptist church beside his home, and I will never forget the sight of him passionately and lovingly encouraging the people to not let fear stop them from really living. He looked sharp in his blue suit, but as I looked down I saw that he was preaching barefoot, his disfigured feet unable to fit into any kind of regular shoes.

When I had met him a few days before, he had given me his first gift—acceptance. But in that moment at the church, he gave me a second gift: the deep realization that the world doesn't need any more perfect people demanding our adulation. What the world needs are more broken people that love without condition.

While I had known for some time that I would never be one of the "perfect people" of this world, I still exerted great effort to show only my best, secretly hating myself for all the ways in which I felt I didn't measure up. But here was Kandume, his whole body, voice, and countenance shouting out a message that echoed the words of Mother Teresa: "In this life, we cannot do great things. We can only do small things with great love." I had never met Mother Teresa, but I had met Kandume.

Throughout the next ten days or so, I watched this man as much as I could. When I greeted him each morning and asked him how he was, his answer was always the same. With his gravelly voice and wonderful Namibian accent, he replied wistfully: "Still standing, still standing."

Kandume had limped through his life loving people simply, and walking alongside him those ten days changed me. What I didn't realize was that he still had more gifts to give me, though he gave no hint of what they were, or indeed that they even existed. In fact, I think he himself may have been unaware of the gifts he had yet to give, because he was so uncalculating and genuine that his offerings simply flowed out of who he was.

One day after lunch, everyone else had rushed off to their responsibilities and we found ourselves together, unhurried and alone.

I asked him about life as a young man growing up in the apartheid era of South Africa. He shared several stories and mentioned his work as a floor washer, for which he was paid a few pennies a day.

"Because we were not considered human, we were treated inhumanly by some, including beatings and abuses of many kinds." He said it without a hint of anger or angst, but not without passion. It was the first time I was ever ashamed of my skin, though I know that was not at all Kandume's intention.

I had to ask the question that was burning a hole through my heart: "Pastor Kandume, how can you treat me with such love and acceptance after going through all of that at the hands of people who looked just like me? Don't I remind you of them, of those days and those experiences?"

"Sam," he said quietly, "if I was going to let those experiences kill me, I would have died a long time ago. Life is too important to have our joy stolen by unforgiveness." His attitude again reminded me of Mother Teresa saying, "Yesterday is gone. Tomorrow has not yet come. We have only today. Let us begin." I had heard Kandume preach a sermon in the church, but here he was living a life's worth of sermons right in front of me.

Our days together were quickly coming to an end and I felt very sad about that. I did have a little plan, though, and that was to scrape together a bit of the money I had with me and leave it with Kandume to cover some of the expenses of our stay. Before I went to bed that last night, I got an envelope and put some cash in it. On the outside of the envelope I wrote a note to Kandume and his wife, thanking and encouraging them as best I could. I knew that the next morning we would be leaving and I wanted to give this small gift to Kandume privately.

Well, before I knew it, the next morning had arrived and we were all saying our goodbyes. The whole group was gathered, along with some of the folks from the church and community. Short speeches were made, as well as expressions of gratitude from all concerned. As the crowd dispersed, Kandume nodded to me and motioned for me to follow him into his house. He asked me to sit in his living room and he brought me a glass of cool water.

"Sam, I want to talk with you and pray with you before you leave here today to begin the rest of your journey," he said. So that is what we did. We talked together, we prayed for each other, and then he stood up and came over and gave me one of those patented Kandume bear hugs.

I figured this would be a good time to fish that envelope out of my inside breast pocket. I looked down momentarily to find it, and when I looked back up I was surprised. I was not the only one in the room pulling an envelope out of his pocket! Here was a man of very humble means, sacrificing so that he could bless me as I went on my way. Our eyes met and we both realized at the same time what the other was up to. We chuckled as we reached out to each other, exchanging our envelopes. We shared another hug, and then I walked outside, got into the truck, and drove off.

I never saw Kandume again.

The next day, after reading his message to me on the outside of the envelope, I opened it carefully. Inside were several bills, as well as a handful of coins. Kandume had obviously not opened his wallet to carefully pick out one or two bills. Instead, he had opened his heart and, in his uncalculated and genuine way, simply lived out his generosity yet again. As I sat there in that moment, I thought about driving back to Kandume's city to return this money to him. But I knew he would not want me to do that. Instead, I used it to help people along the rest of my journey through Namibia—paying school fees for a student who had to stay home for lack of funds, buying some groceries for a hungry family, and purchasing a pair of sneakers for a young man with no shoes. I think Kandume would have wanted it that way.

I received an e-mail from a friend a year later, telling me that Kandume had died suddenly. He had finished his travels on this earth unexpectedly, but then, he had always been ready to stay or go at a moment's notice.

Thinking back now, three things about Kandume's life set him apart from the ordinary. First of all, one felt courageous around him. His zest for life was contagious and his joy in the midst of everyday tasks was unforgettable.

Secondly, his lack of bitterness freed him to make the most of every moment and every interaction. If anyone had a reason to live in unforgiveness, it would have been Kandume. He had not been hurt by only one or two people, but by a whole way of life that had loudly exclaimed that he was worthless because his skin was so dark. But Kandume was too busy loving people to examine and re-examine the hurts committed against him. He was occupied with overcoming evil with good, and he was more than occasionally successful at it.

Finally, Kandume lived a generous life. He was generous emotionally, spiritually, and physically. He gave and gave and gave some more. Though not financially wealthy, he was one of the richest men I have ever met, before or since. And in spite of his own modest lifestyle, he considered it a privilege to help a fellow traveler. I honestly don't remember how much money was in the envelope he gave me that day, and all of it has long since been spent there in Namibia. I only know that the time I spent with Kandume has made me a rich man, one that wants to be a Kandume in someone else's life.

Chapter Two

The Stardust Roller Rink
(The Place to Be)

As improbable as it sounds, my journey to Africa and encounter with Kandume were set in motion by a trip to a roller skating rink decades earlier. An unstoppable chain of events had begun to unfold in my life, though it was certainly not engineered or designed by me.

I was fourteen years old at the time and my life seemed a little crazy. The boredom of junior high school in general (and ninth grade geography in particular) was juxtaposed with the pain of experiencing my parent's marriage slowly disintegrating.

It was 12:01 p.m. on April 2, 1977, and most everyone had filed out of the science class at Cloverdale Junior High School. My best friend Warren saw me sitting motionless in my chair, holding my long moping face in my hands.

"What's wrong, Sammy boy?" he asked as he walked over my way.

Being fourteen, there was one particular issue that I had on my mind a lot. "Warren, it's very simple," I responded. "I NEED A GIRLFRIEND!"

"Oh yeah," Warren replied, "I do know what you're talkin' about. But I've got good news! By the end of this month, I *know* that we are both gonna have girlfriends!"

Twenty-eight days later, at 12:01 p.m. on April 30, 1977, most everyone had once again filed out of the science class at Cloverdale Junior High. My best friend Warren saw me sitting motionless in my chair, again holding my long moping face in my hands. But now, Warren was sitting motionless in his own chair, holding his long moping face, too.

I started, "I thought you said..."

"Yeah, yeah, I know," Warren answered, cutting me off. He had real determination in his voice as he suddenly stood up straight and tall. "This calls for drastic measures, Sam."

He looked me right in the eye.

"You're not suggesting..." My voice trailed off at the very thought of it.

"Yes, Sam, I am suggesting... the Stardust Roller Skating Rink!"

The Stardust Roller Rink was famous in our part of the Canadian universe, at least among fourteen-year-olds. I imagined that if I ever dared to go to the place, my life would never be the same again. How true this prophecy would prove to be—but not for the reason I was thinking.

Fast forward to Friday night. I skated the rounds on that cold cement floor, trying desperately to keep vertical as I weaved and bobbed to the sounds of K.C. and the Sunshine Band. Suddenly the lighting in the rink changed dramatically and the big sign in the corner flashed those two ominous words that I both anticipated and feared—"Couples Only!"

I skated into the "holding tanks," heart pounding as I approached what I anticipated would be the first of many brush-offs that night.

"Uh, excuse me," I stammered to a girl, "would you like to s-s-skate?" I lowered my eyes in an attempt to hide my impending disappointment, but her positive answer instead caused my face to break out in a big smile as my hands simultaneously broke out in a nasty case of the sweats. Just moments later, we were circling the rink together, talking and laughing and enjoying the moment. She didn't even seem to mind my sweaty hand problem too much, though I confess that I thought I was going to lose her a few times around the corners because of it!

That girl, Karen, and I became real friends. We started spending time together, going to movies or skating, just having fun and getting to know each other.

I have such vivid memories of the first time I went to her house for dinner. As her dad said a prayer before dinner, he spoke like he was really talking with God. Wow, that weirded me out! I could handle the occasional little poem at meal time: "Thank you for the food we eat, thank you for the world so sweet," but this was completely different. Before long, I was going to church with her family on Sundays, and that was pretty different, too. People really got into it—singing, praying, lifting their hands. It was so different from the church I had sporadically attended as a child, where the main two activities of the congregation seemed to be yawning and checking one's watch.

Six weeks after meeting Karen at the roller rink, we sat at McDonald's having a Coke. In the midst of our conversation, Karen became a little more serious and asked, "Sam, are you a Christian?" No one had ever asked me that before.

"Uh, yes," I answered, stalling for time as I considered my response. Finally, I replied with firmer conviction: "I was born in Canada, so yes, I'm a Christian." Karen began to laugh so hard that she almost fell off her yellow plastic chair, and I was really offended.

"What are you laughing about?" I asked, wearing my best scowl.

"Sam, being born in Canada doesn't make you a Christian," she said. "Having a life-changing encounter and relationship with Jesus Christ makes you a Christian."

I still felt a little offended as I sipped on my Coke, but I was curious, too. Could a person actually "get to know" Jesus?

Little did I know how much this one question and this one quest would change not only the direction of my life, but also the people I would meet along the way. As I sat at that McDonald's restaurant, there was no way to foresee that my journey would one day allow me to cross paths with a young woman named Valencia. Her story is extraordinary, and so is the question she wants to ask you...

CHAPTER THREE

VALENCIA
(Surprise at the Amphitheatre)

There we were, about five hundred people gathered at a natural outdoor amphitheatre. It was one of those magical evenings when the warm evening air wraps around you like a favourite pair of flannel pyjamas. Not too hot, not too cold... just right.

We were watching a stirring presentation by a drama and dance group. Somehow, they managed to communicate deep truths about life without using a single word. It was as if their hearts had a direct line to our hearts. Their movements and faces spoke volumes. It was all very gentle, very natural, very unforced. It drew us in.

As we watched attentively, I noticed a funny optical illusion. One girl in the second row of the dance group was standing in such a way, and at such an angle, that she appeared to have only one leg. It was a very unusual illusion, unintended no doubt. She was a wonderful dancer, among the best on stage. Of course, I began to watch her more intently, waiting for the visual image to dissolve into reality.

It never did.

Honestly, I was a little taken aback when I realized that this was no illusion. It's not that I didn't think she belonged on stage. Actually, my shock was due to the fact that she so clearly did belong there. Unexpectedly, I realized that she had an old wooden crutch under one arm. I thought it strange that I had not noticed it up until now. She moved so naturally, and with such confidence. The crutch was neither highlighted nor hidden; it was simply part of her reality.

Every person in the dance group was excellent. Each one was a pleasure to watch. But this one person reached me at a deeper level. I was glued to her because of the way she communicated hope and life and freedom. Why and how was she impacting me like this? Did I see the potential of my own limitations being shattered as I watched the celebration before me? Did I feel the stirring of renewed hope for areas of my life that had left me crippled, albeit in less obvious ways?

I found out later that her name was Valencia. Sixteen years old, she had lost her right leg in a car accident when she was only seven. A high school senior now, she loved to dance, and it showed.

We met her the next day and I was struck by her timidity. She was friendly but tentative, seemingly unsure of herself. I was reminded that while we reveal our truth in different shades and to differing extents, we are all a mixture of boldness and uncertainty, peace and anxiety.

Valencia's humanity was just one more reason to appreciate her. She wasn't some prima donna who had overcome the odds to great fame and fortune. She was a young person with all the normal insecurities and challenges. On top of that, she had been given some unique hills to climb. As she journeyed onward, though, she did so passionately, joyfully, and authentically. She unknowingly set an example for the rest of us.

Valencia had every reason to want to hide in the crowd. She had every reason to sit in the back row. But instead, she danced.

You have probably never met Valencia, nor are you likely to. But will you take a moment and imagine her in your mind right now? Dark eyes. Compassionate smile. Picture her coming up to you, her one leg and her old wooden crutch leaving a unique set of footprints across this earth. As she greets you, you too are taken with her thoughtful, gentle demeanour. Then out of the blue, she says to you, "The music is playing, but it plays for such a short time."

"Excuse me?" you reply, slightly taken aback.

"May I ask you a question?" she says gently.

"Well, yes, I... yes, sure," you respond, surprised at your own mixture of hesitation and expectation.

Using just six words, she asks you a question that has the potential to change the trajectory of your life.

"What is keeping you from dancing?"

CHAPTER FOUR

DECISION AT THE DOCK
(Four Minutes Is All It Will Take)

My teen years were a very turbulent time. After Karen told me that being born in Canada was no guarantee I was a Christian, I felt unsettled. I had never thought of myself as a serious Christian, but I had always figured that God was out there somewhere, and my job was simply to do the best I could. If I did more good things than bad, maybe it would all work out in the end. Mostly I just tried to avoid the whole issue—"If you don't bother me, God, I won't bother You." But now, thanks to Karen, I had this nagging thought that maybe there was more to faith than just "God... out there somewhere."

Being fourteen years old, I was soon on to other things—namely, my budding friendship with Karen. We were spending a lot of time together, and it was fun having a regular partner at the Stardust Roller Rink.

One day, she invited me to a youth weekend at a local camp. The teenagers from her church were all heading there for three days, and since the camp was built on lakefront property, there would be swimming and water skiing. Hmmm... beach, water skiing, and a girlfriend for the weekend. It was a no-brainer: where do I sign up?

There are few conversations that one can clearly remember three decades after they have taken place, but the one I had that Friday afternoon as I packed for my weekend away was an unusual one. At that stage of my life, things weren't going too well. School wasn't great. Friendships weren't great. Heck, I didn't even like myself most of the time. But there was one good thing I could always count on: my family. That's why this particular conversation was so important and so memorable, even thirty years later. It had everything to do with my "one good thing."

I was in my room, getting a few belongings together for the big weekend, when my mom came to the door and asked if we could talk. I nodded as I threw my socks and an extra pair of pants into a backpack, my mind a million miles away.

"Sam, you probably know that your dad and I have not been doing well for a long time," she said. "Well, we've decided to get a divorce and one of us is moving out in two weeks. You have until then to decide who you want to live with."

Those three sentences were like an emotional baseball bat to my head. I was stunned, but I tried to hide my shock by turning my back to my mom and muttering some unrecognizably garbled response.

Later that afternoon, we met at Karen's church and fifty teens and leaders jumped on an old school bus. We made our way down to The Firs, a camp in nearby Bellingham, Washington. That night, we gathered together in the main lodge to hear a speaker. If you offered me a million dollars right now, I couldn't tell you what he spoke about. It's not that he was uninteresting; it's just that I was still reeling from the news that the one good thing in my life was being torn apart. My mom's words kept echoing in my mind: "We've decided to get a divorce... you've got two weeks... we've decided to get a divorce... you've got two weeks." Even after all these years, I can still feel the hopelessness of that moment.

I sat there, not listening to the speaker, my eyes filling up with tears. I lowered my head to try to stay under the radar of the other kids. I knew what teenaged boys did when they saw other teenaged boys crying. I'd witnessed it once at my junior high school, and it wasn't pretty. I didn't wish that on anybody—least of all me.

In that moment, I came up with a plan. I remembered our gym teacher telling us how important proper breathing was, and that a person would die after only four minutes of oxygen deprivation. The lake was only fifty meters from where I was sitting, and I put two and two together. As soon as I could sneak out of that room without anyone noticing, I would run down to the lake, run along the dock and then dive in and swim down three meters. If I could hold onto the piling underwater for only four minutes, I would never have to experience this kind of pain again. Ever.

By this time, I was sitting there with my head in my hands, my eyes red and swollen, and tears and snot running down my face. I was a mess. I knew that at any moment, the other kids were going to take notice of me. The mocking was about to begin, but now I didn't care, because I had my four-minute plan.

The speaker finished his talk and I prepared to make my exit. Some of the kids noticed my red face and started to come towards me. I braced myself for what was about to come. They gathered around me, asking what was wrong. I couldn't answer because I was crying too hard. They moved in closer, surrounding me. This was going to be even worse than I thought. Then the leader of this little pack did something completely bizarre— he dropped to his knees and began to pray.

He began to pray for me.

The other teens joined in too, some putting a hand on my shoulder or on my knee as I sat there, still sobbing. Those kids had every reason to laugh at me, mock me, and ridicule me—but they didn't. They did the one thing that was completely unnatural (supernatural?) for teenagers to do for a messed-up, red-eyed, snotty-faced, bawling fourteen-year-old boy: they loved me.

After ten minutes or so, I was calmed down enough to explain the situation. After they understood the reason behind my tears, they prayed yet again. There was something powerful in the prayers of these teens, something that gave me hope. In the midst of what I experienced as total darkness, these people had lit a single candle. It wasn't everything I wanted, but it was everything I needed. If genuine, unselfish, nothing-in-it-for-me love could exist among these young people, God had to be behind it. And if God would be so bold as to embrace me through these people, then there was hope—even now, even for me.

At this moment, I had no capacity to love others—I didn't even have the ability to love myself. Yet hope remained. During my short life, I had heard the phrase "Jesus loves you" from people on the street and from talking heads on TV, but it had always rung very hollow to me. Besides, if God was just "out there somewhere" and I was left on my own to "try my best," what difference did He make?

In this moment, though, Jesus loving me was not a tired turn of phrase, but the one life raft I had on the sea of hopelessness. It wasn't just the wishful thinking of a desperate soul either, for these kids around me were not acting normally. They were flesh and blood, in my space, living out Jesus' love to me—loving me when they had no good reason on earth to do so. That love began to change me. It began to change the way I saw people and situations.

CHAPTER FIVE

DARK EYES UNDER THE TABLE
(What the Heck is Under There?)

In the heart of the South American rainforest, on the banks of the mighty Amazon River, a wise traveler must garner all his wits to answer the timeless question: "What's for dinner?" When hunger pangs seized me in Iquitos, Peru, I could have done worse than land in a flame-broiled chicken joint.

I had flown to Peru to work with an aid organization, and I was scheduled to start the next day. Little did I know that God had already begun to work on me. Life-changing events were about to happen in that run-of-the-mill chicken restaurant.

I sat with the director of the team, ordered some food, and discussed the plan for the upcoming week of projects. Suddenly, out of the corner of my eye, I saw something dart from table to table.

Way too big to be a rat, I thought. Perhaps a small dog, begging for crumbs and bones?

Hey, there it went again. Could that be a little...? Before I could finish my thought, whatever it was had nose-dived under my table and was clutching my foot. Fear and embarrassment made my heart skip a beat. Leaning down to get a better look, I realized that it was a little boy.

The skinny kid looked no more than five or six, about the same age as my own son, whom I had left safely back in Canada.

Yes, he was definitely holding onto my foot. Although everything in me wanted to recoil, his dark shining eyes held me in their grip. I saw such hopelessness there, but also such burning life.

As my eyes adjusted to the dim light under the table, I noticed the boy clenching a small wooden box in his free hand. A dirty rag hung out of it. Suddenly, I understood: he was a shoeshine boy.

This scurrying from table to table was no children's game, but the grim cunning of survival. If the restaurant manager caught the boy, he would chase him out with a broom, and there would be no supper that night. But if the child managed to sneak to my table, he might earn a few pennies to buy food. My boat shoes were not "shoeshine-able," but I found myself giving the boy a nod of approval anyway. He set to work, snapping that towel like a true pro. He soon completed a wonderful job—at least for boat shoes.

I slipped some money into his hand and he bolted away as quickly as he had arrived. I never saw him again.

Many years have passed since that night, and I often find myself thinking of those dark shining eyes. Why didn't I invite the little boy to sit with me and share my meal? Why didn't I take him around the corner to buy him some new pants and a decent shirt? It had all happened so fast. And then he was gone.

Little kids shouldn't have to worry about where their next meal will come from. They shouldn't have to dart from place to place, in fear of being driven away with a broom. They should be able to laugh and play and learn beyond the shadow of a doubt that they have unlimited value in the eyes of their heavenly Father.

I know I missed my opportunity to really help that little shoeshine boy. He is a reminder to me that we have opportunities to make a difference every day in the lives of people, if only we will take the chance. Because of that little boy, I remember that I have never regretted the times I have been generous, but I have often regretted the times I have turned away in selfishness.

CHAPTER SIX

MOVING AHEAD IN FITS AND STARTS
(What Do You Mean, 'God Has Other Plans'?)

That shoeshine boy and I had a few things in common. As I grew up, I had tried to rely on hard work and smarts to make my way in the world. That's why the love and acceptance I experienced at that teen camp had such an impact on me. It wasn't about people responding to my best efforts, it was about people pouring hope, acceptance, and love on me when I was at my worst.

I came home from that camp with more than just a flicker of hope that things would get better. Maybe if I prayed hard enough, my family would stay together. I remember staying up all night, guitar in hand, singing and praying and asking God to keep my family together. By six the next morning, I was pretty sure that things would work out. I mean, isn't there some rule that God has to answer your prayer if you stay up all night asking for it?

Apparently no such rule existed.

My mom did eventually leave, taking my older sister and younger brother with her. My dad did his best to keep things going, but that dinner table had a lot of empty chairs around it. Because there were just two of us now, there was always more food than we could eat—yet I'd never felt so empty.

Months and years rolled by and my friendship with God was anything but stable. Karen and I had broken up and I stopped going to church with her. I didn't stop believing, but I stopped talking with God and, more importantly, I stopped listening.

Achievement became my highest priority. Lead in the school play? Check. President of the student council? Check. Girlfriend du jour? Check. Anything to try to numb the pain and emptiness? Check.

Yes, I had experienced God's life-changing love, but sometimes His changes happen over a lifetime. I wanted instant fulfillment and I needed something for the pain. I was spending my days at the drive-thru window of life—I wanted it all and I wanted it now. It served a purpose for a while, but it didn't nourish me.

My roots were getting shallower by the month, and I was uneasy. Sadly, I had forgotten where to turn for help.

As I look back, I see that the most important things are not things at all. It's the people that impacted me, for better and for worse. Oh, I have definitely chosen my own path through life, whether it has been a superhighway (there have been a few) or a dead end street (there have been many). But the signposts along the way have not been green metallic placards, but flesh and blood people who have waved and encouraged me to go with them this way or that.

By this time, I was out of high school and attending Music College. My faith was on the backburner (the farthest back of the backburners) and I was dating a girl named Michele. Things were going along pretty smoothly until she phoned me one afternoon and told me that she had to talk to me in person. She had news—something very personal that couldn't be shared over the phone.

"It's going to change everything," she said. I was pretty nervous.

That night we met at her place. She grabbed my hands and said, "Sam, I've become a Christian. My best friend at school helped me to understand that God is on our side. He doesn't want us to run from Him, he wants us to run to Him."

I'm embarrassed to say that I had never told Michele about God or about my inconsistent relationship with Him. By this time, I had fallen back into running my own show, and God was definitely at arm's length. Now suddenly here He was, boldly showing up in the life of my girlfriend. Talk about a conundrum. It was like having Jesus show up at your front door when you're right in the middle of a house party. "Oh, hi Jesus," you say as you step outside to talk to Him, quickly slamming the door to keep the noise, the mess, and the party-goers out of sight. "Ah, hmm, now's not... the... best time, but ah... hey, thanks for stopping by!"

"Sam," He replies, "I'd like to spend some time with you. I've missed you."

"Oh Jesus, if You only knew, You wouldn't..."

"But I do know... and I would. In fact, more than ever."

I started to hang out with Michele's Christian friends and even showed up at their church a few times. It reminded me of being at the weekend camp a few years before. Once again, I was expecting rejection, but what I received was acceptance. I particularly remember going over to the home of one of the people from her church, a guy named Michael Hansen. We would sit around the family room with his parents, asking a million different questions about faith, life, God, and Jesus. I'm sure now that some of my questions must have sounded pretty stupid, but you would never have known it from Mr. and Mrs. Hansen's response. They modeled hope and stability (which I really needed) and they shared acceptance and love (which I needed most of all). I got connected into the community of their church in Langley, British Columbia. Like a seed being nurtured by sun, rain, and good soil, I began to put down roots. Michele and I eventually went our separate ways, both knowing that God had other plans for us. This time I was stronger in my faith and I had a support system in that community that was not dependant on my girlfriend.

What I didn't know was that the real adventures were just beginning to unfold. Sometimes these adventures would be geographically-based, like trekking through the outskirts of Kathmandu, Nepal, or navigating a kayak away from irate hippos on the Zambezi River in southwest Africa. Mostly though, these adventures involved people—incredibly courageous people with spirits that inspired me to live more dangerously in the safe, strong hands of God.

Chapter Seven

The Empty Margarine Container
(I Tried Not to Stare. Really.)

The slums of Lima, Peru are a dangerous and unpleasant place. A visitor's sense of sight and smell are overwhelmed as you walk through the dusty, garbage-strewn streets.

I was there with a group of North American teens and their leaders to partner with local Christians, sharing our faith and helping with the construction of their small church. It was our third day in and we were mixing cement by hand under the hot Peruvian sun.

Three one-hundred-pound bags, three wheelbarrows of rocks, and three wheelbarrows of sand, mixed with "mass agua, mass agua" ("more water"), and put into buckets, were lifted onto the roof and poured. Then we did it all over again. And again. And again. It reminded me of my five-year-old daughter making cookie dough for her easy-bake oven, except on a much larger scale and with a much brighter light bulb.

The 100-degree heat was starting to take its toll on all of us—even the three no-neck American football players, with muscles in places where I didn't have places, were melting in the sun.

As a leader, I was trying to set an example, but the truth is that my mind and body were on completely opposite sides of the debate as to what exactly that example should be.

Then I saw her.

She stood about 4'3", stooped over, a baby slung across her shoulders. Her back was to me and I could see only the little baby, her brightly-coloured coat and two long braids protruding out of her thick-knit hat.

She turned my way and I discovered the deeply-lined face of an old woman and a dark, empty place where her right eye used to be. Immediately I looked away, not wanting to stare. Well, actually, I'm embarrassed to say that I did want to stare. I just didn't want to get caught doing it.

I watched as she hobbled into our group, and I saw that she had an empty margarine container in her hand.

Oh, no, I thought to myself. *We're already behind schedule and now this scary-looking lady is going to beg from our group, upset the girls, and put us even further behind.* I'm not proud of what my inside voice was saying, but I can't pretend it didn't exist either.

The old woman walked among us, neither holding out the margarine container nor attempting to make any kind of contact with us. She definitely got my attention when she slowly walked to the gravel pile and her already-stooped body hunched down even further as she used the old plastic container to scoop some rocks up. She then slowly and agonizingly walked over to where the cement was being mixed and she poured her tiny pile of rocks out on the cement mixing pile. The big American guys were going back and forth dumping wheelbarrows of rocks and sand and she began to go back and forth dumping one tiny margarine container at a time.

At first, it seemed almost laughable. A chuckle rose in my throat about the same moment that tears came to my eyes. One by one, the guys noticed what she was doing. Suddenly their tired bodies were filled with a new strength as they too started to give everything they had to the task at hand.

You know, that woman had every excuse not to give of herself. She was elderly and she was weak and she was literally half-blind. She had a baby grandchild to look after and she was stooped over. There were so many younger and stronger people who could do the job better and faster, and yet she wanted her love and sweat poured into the foundation of that church.

Unlike so many of us, she wasn't thinking about all the reasons that she couldn't make a difference, she was thinking about the one reason that she could: God was giving her an opportunity.

We couldn't speak two words of each other's language and yet her actions communicated a life-changing message.

I believe that even with new bodies in Heaven, we'll be able to recognize each other, and when I see her, I'm going to rush up to her and call her by name.

I'm going to call her "Faithful."

CHAPTER EIGHT

THE EARLY YEARS AROUND THE WORLD
(Europe, Africa, and Southeast Asia)

My friendship with God was changing my life. In my early twenties, I developed a deep desire to make a difference in the lives of others. I quit my job with a financial services company to work at a youth centre with street kids in a rough part of Metro Vancouver. The kids were broken by life, and sometimes they tried to break us youth workers, too. I remember one young man who had burnt all the hair off his face—eyebrows, eyelashes, everything. He pulled a knife on me one night, promising to cut me into nice even pieces. The other street kids gathered around me, forming a human shield. One of the biggest guys walked up to my attacker and simply commanded him to "drop it." He did.

One day, a co-worker introduced me to a new volunteer, Rita. *She seems nice,* I thought, but I wasn't looking for a relationship. Five months later, we were engaged, and five months after our engagement, we were married. When it's right, it's right!

Shortly after the wedding, doctors told Rita that she would never have children. But five months after getting married (what was it with us and five months?!), the little blue strip lit up like a neon sign to say, "Don't believe everything you hear!" Eight months later, Tanaya Joelle was born. About two years after that came our second daughter, Dana Marie.

I moved on from the youth centre to work with Youth for Christ, an international Christian organization started by Billy Graham in the 1940s. At first, I spoke and did concerts at local events, a church youth group here or a special event there. Within a few years, I was participating in outreaches across Canada, and then the overseas trips began. The first international ministry was a tour of ten cities across the United Kingdom with the Salvation Army. Soon after that came an invitation to go to Namibia, Africa. Then it was on to Singapore.

Rita did an incredible job keeping the home fires burning, but it was very hard on her. I was a ball of nerves before long trips and a lump of exhaustion after them. In spite of that, we saw God doing in young people what He had done in our own lives as teenagers—giving hope and new direction through a life-changing relationship with Him.

After being away for five or six weeks at a time, I would come home and we would work at reintegrating our lives. We had a strong sense that this was what we were to be doing. Once in a while, Rita and the kids came along, like on the second trip to Singapore. We had a nine-month-old in tow now: our son, Taylor Samuel. The kids made quite a splash in Singapore. People thought that Taylor was Buddha himself with his round belly and chubby cheeks. There was never a shortage of people pinching those cheeks and even rubbing his little baby belly!

One day, we took the kids to the Singapore Zoo and the girls got their photo taken with an orangutan. Shyly, a group of Asian tourists asked if they could have their picture with five-year-old Dana, who had red hair and porcelain white skin. They actually lined up to get their photo taken with her.

"Look, Mom!" she exclaimed. "They think I'm Shirley Temple!" We all laughed and agreed that next time we would sell tickets for the privilege of having photos taken with our Dana.

While the family remained in Singapore, I flew north to Burma (Myanmar) for a ten-day outreach. I traveled there with a group of Asian Christians, but as the only Caucasian I stuck out like a sore thumb. One night, my co-worker came into our hotel room in Rangoon (it was illegal to stay in a Burmese person's home), and exclaimed, "We need to pray! The secret police know your whole schedule already and they will have spies recording every word you say at every place you speak!"

I was not so afraid for my own safety as I was for the Burmese who were with me. The military government could simply make them disappear if they perceived that we were a threat to them in any way.

At one of the concerts in Burma, there was a group of thirty-five young people in the audience who were all blind. I found out that they had been abandoned children picked up off the street by a caring group of Christian women who started an orphanage and school for them.

Just before I was to speak, a person came up to lead everyone in a few worship songs. Here we were in one of the poorest countries in the world. The first three rows were filled with all the children, teens, and young adults from the orphanage for the blind. These kids had almost everything going against them: poverty, physical disability, and abandonment by their parents. But what song did they sing from the bottom of their hearts with huge smiles across their faces?

God is so good
God is so good
God is so good
He's so good to me!

I love Him so
I love Him so

I love Him so
He's so good to me!

For them, experiencing the powerful love of God and the powerful God-inspired love of their "house-mothers" was enough. They knew that they were blessed no matter what anyone else thought or said.

After the service, the leader of the school asked me if the kids could come up and "take a look" at me. I wasn't sure what it meant for blind kids to look at me, but I agreed without hesitation. They formed a line and one by one they shook my hand and then gently ran their fingers over my face to form a mental picture of me. The best part was watching them trying to suppress their giggles when they felt my nose, which was (and still is!) considerably more "abundant" than their own petite Asian noses!

When I think of these young people in Burma, I actually feel sad for the teens of rich North American and western European countries. These Burmese youth challenged my understanding of what it means to be rich and what it means to be poor.

In the western world, we often talk about karma. Some think of it as a happy and magical math equation for keeping our lives joyful and (mostly) problem-free. The difficulty is that if we take this concept seriously, then a blind, abandoned baby that is starving in the street deserves what she gets because she must have been horribly selfish in her previous life. The concept of karma can seduce us into justifying our own self-centeredness and lack of compassion.

The women who started that orphanage and picked those children up off the street did not believe in karma. They believed in laying down their lives to serve others.

A huge motivator for me is that I believe God will one day have a conversation with us about the people He brought across our path during our lifetime. In the Bible, Jesus tells about a future conversation that He will have with those who care enough to make a difference:

> "'For I was hungry and you gave me something to eat, I was thirsty and you gave me something to drink, I was a stranger and you invited me in, I needed clothes and you clothed me, I was sick and you looked after me, I was in prison and you came to visit me.'
>
> "Then the righteous will answer him, 'Lord, when did we see you hungry and feed you, or thirsty and give you something to drink? When did we see you a stranger and invite you in, or needing clothes and clothe you? When did we see you sick or in prison and go to visit you?'
>
> "The King will reply, 'I tell you the truth, whatever you did for one of the least of these brothers of mine, you did for me.' (Matthew 25:35-40)

I am so thankful that there are hundreds of thousands of people around the world who make sacrifices every day to make a difference in the lives of those who are orphaned, hungry, or hopeless. No one asks for their autograph or takes their photo for a magazine cover. They are mostly unnoticed and ignored, but their lives count.

I want to be one of those people.

CHAPTER NINE

TWENTY MINUTES TO SAY "I LOVE YOU"
(How Could One So Little Teach Us So Much?)

After Rita and I married in 1986, she began experiencing a lot of abdominal pain. We saw doctor after doctor and she took medication after medication. Eventually, she was diagnosed with "you'vegotsomekindofaproblemthatwcan't-figureoutbutweknowyou'renevergonnahaveababyitis." It was only four months into our marriage, and one of our major dreams was already crushed. Even though we had planned to wait a few years before trying to have a child, we were heartbroken. Interestingly enough, it was just three weeks after that ironclad declaration from the experts that we found out we were expecting our first child, Tanaya. Dana Marie Rowland followed just twenty-one months later.

Tanaya and Dana were soon seven and five, and after another round of "youcan'thaveanymoreexceptmaybeifyoutakethisdrug-itis," Rita had a prescription that was supposed to help us get pregnant. She was to begin taking it after her next cycle, but her next cycle never came because we were pregnant again.

"Daddy," my daughter Tanaya asked, "can we have a little boy this time, please?"

"Well, sweetie," I answered, "you can't really put in an order like that."

"Daddy, if it can't be a boy, then can it be a puppy?" she said. I laughed so hard that all I could get out was, "I'll see what we can do, honey."

A few months later, Rita and I went for an ultrasound to look at our little "pup." We got a note from our doctor the next day saying, "Sam and Rita, I've seen your ultrasound results. You're expecting a beautiful baby boy. He's due in three months time and he's absolutely perfect!"

Some friends of ours, Randy and Darla, were expecting their first child and went for their ultrasound around the same time. But instead of getting a note the next day like we did, they got a telephone call from the doctor himself.

"Randy and Darla, please come down to my office right away," he said. "Don't worry about an appointment. Can you come down now?"

As our friends sat with their doctor, he explained that just like us, they were expecting a beautiful baby boy. And just like us, he was due in about three months time. The difference was that his little heart was not developing properly—he had a condition known as hypoplastic left heart syndrome.

Now it was decision time.

Option A was abortion. It could be arranged right away and that little boy would be gone by the next afternoon. Option B was to have that little baby and just hope for the best, though the doctor explained that he didn't think the baby would survive for very long after he was born if there was no intervention. But there was also option C. In this third scenario, their son would be born naturally, and within hours of his birth, he would be taken into surgery for a new experimental procedure that had shown some recent success. The doctor confirmed, however, that there were no guarantees.

He told them to go home and think about it, but Randy and Darla just squeezed each other's hands and told the doctor that they wanted option C.

Three months later, Rita and I welcomed Taylor Samuel Rowland into our world. Two weeks after that, Randy and Darla welcomed little Bryce into theirs. They held him in their arms for twenty short minutes and then the nurses came and said, "It's time." They took Bryce away and began to connect him to tubes and wires in preparation for surgery.

When I heard the results of the operation, I was so impacted that I wrote a song for Bryce and for his parents. It's called *Twenty Minutes to Say "I Love You."*

> *The doctor knew there was a problem*
> *Though his birth was still at least three months away*
> *His tiny heart, oh it was struggling*
> *The doctor offered no guarantees that day*
>
> *Fourteen weeks and three days later*
> *Little Bryce was finally born*
> *The surgical team was prepped and ready*
> *But they gave his parents time with their firstborn*
>
> *And they had twenty minutes to say "I love you"*
> *Twenty minutes to hold him in their arms*
> *Those twenty minutes passed like the twinkling of an eye*
> *Then the nurses came to get him and he was gone*
>
> *The operation took much longer*
> *Then they had planned for it to be*
> *The doctor finally came to tell them both the news*
> *It was not news they were ready to receive*
>
> *His little heart was just too broken*
> *There was nothing left to say*

His father fell to his knees, his heart was broken too
But it was broken in a much more painful way

'Cause they had only twenty minutes to say, "I love you"
Twenty minutes to hold him in their arms
In those twenty minutes they spent a lifetime
'Cause in twenty minutes he was gone

I don't know why death has taken their son
When life has brought a little boy to me
But I'll remember the final notes have not yet played
In this unfinished symphony

So I'll take twenty minutes to say "I love you"
Twenty minutes to hold you in my arms
I realize now that even twenty minutes is a gift
So let me simply hold you and tell you how I love you
Every moment that we share is a gift of grace.

I saw Randy and Darla a few weeks after Bryce passed on. They showed me photos of him, wrapped in a blue blanket and wearing a little blue hat. Pictures of Mom holding Bryce. Pictures of Dad holding Bryce. Pictures of Mom and Dad with Bryce. Towards the second half of the little photo album, the pictures changed dramatically. There were photos of Bryce lying in a little white casket, only thirty inches long. It was hard to look at these photos. He looked so perfect. Why was he lying in a casket and not in a cradle like my son? I had no answers, only questions. I ached for Randy and Darla. Silently, deep inside, I felt guilty for having a healthy son.

Some time later, I was reading Psalm 39:4-5 where King David is talking with God. In his usual down-to-earth and honest way, the king of Israel says to the King of the universe:

Show me, O LORD, my life's end
and the number of my days;
let me know how fleeting is my life.

You have made my days a mere handbreadth;
the span of my years is as nothing before you.
Each man's life is but a breath.

I still don't understand how Bryce's life could be measured in hours, while my son Taylor-Sam is now almost fifteen years old. But I do know this: Bryce's too-short visit to this planet is a reminder to me that in the grand scheme of things, our lives are very brief, too.

Some of the people we meet today might have five years left on this planet. Some might have twenty—or even fifty—years left, but one day we will all stand before our Maker. When we do, I believe our first words will be, "It can't be over already. I feel like I was just getting started. It seems like I had just twenty minutes to live my life."

Moments after you find yourself standing on the edge of eternity, God will call you by name and ask you the most important question you have ever been asked, the most important question you will ever be asked.

"My Child," He will ask quietly and slowly, "What did you do with the twenty minutes that I gave you to live?"

There will be many frightened and ashamed people on that day, but God has made a way so that the first day of the rest of your eternity needn't be terrifying. In fact, it can be the most joyful, unbelievably fantastic celebration of your entire existence!

You see, God knew that we would mess things up, live selfishly at times, even hurt each other. That is the price of giving us free will—our own choice to love or not to love, to be generous or to be self-centered. And before we knew or cared about God, He came up with a plan. He would send His own Son to this earth, to become "one of us." His Son would live a perfect and pure life, and then He would allow Himself to take the punishment that was due this world. He would take the pain and suffering upon Himself, even to the point of dying a cruel death on a cross of wood, all to justify God's deep desire to pour forgiveness and love out on those who would humble themselves and come near to Him. Not only that, but three days after dying on that cross, Jesus came back to life. The Bible says that the power that brought Jesus back to life is available to you and me so that we will have the resources to live in a whole new way:

> I pray that your hearts will be flooded with light so that you can understand the confident hope he has given to those he called—his holy people who are his rich and glorious inheritance.
>
> I also pray that you will understand the incredible greatness of God's power for us who believe him. This is the same mighty power that raised Christ from the dead and seated him in the place of honor at God's right hand in the heavenly realms. Now he is far above any ruler or authority or power or leader or anything else—not only in this world but also in the world to come. (Ephesians 1:18-21, NLT)

God is going to ask you that question one day, but the time to figure out your answer is not then—it's right now. When you understand how you want to answer God, you can start living out that answer here and now, one day at a time, by faith. I know how I want to answer Him on that day. When God asks me what I did with my twenty minutes, I want to say, "Lord, I gave my twenty minutes away to you. You made something special of it. You took a lost kid who wanted to drown himself and You filled me with hope. You forgave all my screw-ups and mistakes, over and over again, and You just kept loving me. You never ever gave up on me so I never gave up on myself. You made my life count. Thank you, Father!"

Bryce's short life constantly reminds me that my life is short too, like fireworks exploding in the night sky. I want my life to make a difference. I'm not satisfied with just having my own dreams come true; I want to play a part in making God's dreams come true. He has invited you and me to do just that, but are we too preoccupied with ourselves to notice?

How will you answer Him on that day when He looks you in the eye and asks, "My child, what did you do with the twenty minutes that I gave you?"

> *For we will all stand before God's judgment seat. It is written: 'As surely as I live,' says the Lord, 'every knee will bow before me; every tongue will confess to God.' So then, each of us will give an account of himself to God.* (Romans 14:10-12)

CHAPTER TEN

TUMOURS, TEARS, AND A TICKET TO AFRICA
(Keep Giving It Away)

Around the time she turned thirteen, our daughter Dana began complaining of back pain. After a misdiagnosis or two, it was determined that she had an *osteoid osteoma*, a type of tumour that grows inside or against a bone. Normally, it doesn't pose too much of a threat as it is benign and can be burned out with a laser beam. In Dana's case, however, the tumour was inside a vertebra in the lower part of her back. That made things a little more complicated. If they used a laser in that delicate part of her spine, there was a major risk of spinal cord damage and possible paralysis in her legs. In consultation with the doctors, we decided that it would be safer to remove the tumour with a more conventional type of surgery.

Dana was on a waiting list for some time, but finally we received a call that she could have the operation in the early part of May. There was a problem, though; I was scheduled to leave for South Africa only twelve hours after the surgery start time. I wanted to be with Dana not just on the day of the surgery, but also for her recovery. Sitting down to talk with her, I explained that I was cancelling the trip. Dana would hear none of that.

"Daddy, you need to go. I'll be okay. You need to go and share what God has put on your heart to tell the people there." Reluctantly, I did not cancel the trip. At least I would be with her as she went into surgery and also be there when she came out of the recovery room.

The night before the surgery, we got a phone call. Dana had been bumped from her scheduled surgery the next day because of a patient who had suffered emergency spinal damage in a car accident. Of course, we all understood, and once again I told Dana that I was cancelling my trip.

"Daddy, I will be happier if you go and do this trip," she said. "I'll be here when you get back. I don't want to be the reason that you cancelled. Go and give it everything you've got!"

After discussing it with Rita, we decided that I would continue on as planned. That goodbye at the airport was much harder than most, knowing what was ahead for Dana and for our whole family. I literally felt like I was being pulled in two directions.

Two days later, I arrived in Port Elizabeth, South Africa, where my dear friends Angelique and Antony Jennings had put together some fantastic ministry opportunities at schools, prisons, and churches. We were very busy right off the top, which helped the time pass quickly as I waited the ten days for Dana's new surgery date.

At the end of a great first week, I found myself being interviewed on a Christian radio station in Port Elizabeth. They played songs off my CD and asked me about the tour. The interview went well. With two minutes left before the 10 p.m. newscast, the interviewer asked me one last question: "Sam, please tell our listeners how they can pray for you. What is on your heart tonight?" The response that welled up in me was completely unanticipated. I wept as I told them about my little girl so far away. I felt so drained, so lonely, and so frustrated at my complete inability to make things different for her.

I was empty. I had nothing left to give, and I had seventeen ministry events left where I needed to have *something* in me that I could give away.

The next morning, I went for a walk on the beach. Climbing up on the black volcanic rock that jutted out into the surf, I found freedom and anonymity. The Indian Ocean was powerful, noisy, and alive. The sea spray soaked my face and clothes, and the pounding of the surf more than covered any sounds that I could make. It was the perfect moment to let loose with God. Tears streamed down my face, but no one would ever know since the ocean spray had already soaked me. I cried and yelled out to God, and the deafening crash of the waves made me silent to all except Him. It was almost like the scene from *Forrest Gump*, where Lieutenant Dan has it out with God as he sits in the crow's nest of the Bubba Gump shrimp boat during a typhoon. The only difference was that I wasn't mad at God; I was overwhelmed. Not only was Dana about to have surgery while I was ten thousand miles from home, but Rita and I had been going through a particularly tough time in our relationship. The physical scene around me was a good metaphor for my life at that moment—wild, unpredictable, and most of all, way beyond my control.

On Sunday morning, we arrived early to set up at a Vineyard church in Port Elizabeth. I still had nothing inside me to give and, internally, I started to panic. I went through my normal sound check and got my notes and Bible ready as I prepared to share a message, but I honestly wondered how I would go through with it. I felt as though I were hosting a dinner with no food. The oven was turned on, but only I knew that there was nothing cooking inside it.

It was about five minutes before the start of the service, when an older woman came up and introduced herself. With absolutely no small talk, she looked me in the eye and said, "Sam, you think that you have nothing to give, but you are wrong. It's as if you have a bag of seed strapped to your waist. You think that the bag is empty, but every time that you reach into that bag, God will give you just what you need to share with the people. After you have reached in a few times and given away a few handfuls, you will say to yourself, It's *really empty now*, but if you keep reaching in by faith, God will give you enough for everyone you meet and enough left over for you, too."

I have no idea who that lady was or how she knew what I needed to hear in that moment. I only knew that she spoke the truth. I kept reaching into my empty heart and then reaching out to others. Miraculously, I always had something to give.

Dana's surgery was scheduled for Thursday at 2:00 a.m., South Africa time. Monday and Tuesday crawled by and on Wednesday, time seemed to completely stand still. I stayed up all night Wednesday and Thursday morning calling Rita's cell phone, trying to get through for an update on Dana's progress. I called every fifteen minutes, but Rita's phone had been shut off because she was at the hospital herself, waiting for the operation to be completed so she could get an update from the surgeon.

Finally, at 3:45 a.m., I was able to get through to Rita. The surgery had been a success. The doctors were all very pleased with the outcome. An incredible weight was lifted from my shoulders.

The next day, I called Rita at home, just to get a further update. Miracle of miracles, I had called Rita on her cell and Rita was talking with Dana on the landline. By turning the cell phone around and holding it up to the regular phone, I was able to talk with Dana directly from South Africa to her hospital bed in Vancouver. It wasn't high tech, but it worked!

The rest of the tour in South Africa was wonderful, and I found that I had a new bounce in my step. I couldn't wait to get home to be with Rita, Dana, and the rest of our family.

As life unfolded during those years, I was finally beginning to understand that there are few "perfect" moments where everything is just as we had imagined it would be. In spite of that, we must somehow discover joy and laughter and life in the midst of where we actually are. The key is to ask ourselves how we need to change our thinking or readjust our attitude so that we can experience and convey joy, laughter, and life—right here, right now.

CHAPTER ELEVEN

LANDMINE AREA

(Johannes Kayimbi: Laughter and Tears)

It was 3:52 a.m. as I (and 237 mostly slumbering strangers) travelled through the dark night some 32,000 feet above the earth. I was both restless and exhausted, having spent the past twenty-three hours making my way from Vancouver to London and now on to Johannesburg en route to Windhoek, Namibia. Because this was my very first trip to Africa, I was excited, but also very nervous.

I pulled off my eye cover for the twelfth time and stared blankly ahead. Rolling to my left, I pulled the window shade up a few inches and saw a most glorious sight: the sun was rising over Africa as it had done every morning since creation. For me, though, it was the very first time.

As I drank in the enormous expanse before me, I began to feel very small. It seemed as if all of Africa was laughing at me, asking what I thought I could possibly do to make a difference in this land. If there were a way that I could have turned that plane around at that moment, I surely would have.

Instead, I prayed.

"God, who am I to come to this place? Who am I to think that I can make a contribution that will change lives?" I was somewhat shocked when I sensed a response deep within me.

It was as if God said to me, "Sam, you are asking the wrong question. It is not 'who are you.' The question is who am I? And the answer is this: I am the Lord, and I will make a way for you if you lay down your life to serve the people whom I will bring across your path. Just as Abraham went to a strange land and was used by Me, I will use you for My good and My glory, if you choose to make yourself available. I *am* and I *will.* "

That message left me with both peace and, paradoxically, anxiety. Drifting into a fitful sleep, I knew that whatever was to come was not far off now.

After forty-two hours of travel, my last flight touched down at Hosea Kutako International Airport in Namibia. The adventure was upon me. I was collected at the airport by my new Namibian friend Jos, and we travelled north by 4x4 into the Okavango region, towards the Angolan border.

The plan was for us to conduct assemblies for thousands of teenagers at high schools across the north. I would do concerts and share my story, telling the young people about how God had reached out to me when I hadn't known or even cared about Him. We also gave each student a small booklet called "Knowing God," with a tear-off section that they could use to write to Youth for Christ in their own country and establish a link for follow-up.

We spoke to hundreds and often thousands of students each day. I was overwhelmed by the opportunities, but also by the needs: spiritual, physical, and relational. AIDS was just beginning to take its toll on this desert land and its people.

We were amazed by the response of the young people. They sang with us and they sang for us. They danced and laughed and listened as I shared my heart. I listened carefully to their hearts, too.

At many of the schools, there were American teachers from the Peace Corps. It was always good to touch base with my

American "cousins," but I was always quick to identify myself as a proud Canadian. Being so far away from home, we shared a certain camaraderie that was missing on the North American continent.

One of the Peace Corps teachers informed me that these young people would never write in to Youth for Christ. "They won't buy stamps," she said. "You'll never hear from any of them!" Though discouraged by her comment, I was overwhelmed by a call from the Youth for Christ office in Namibia a few days later. They informed us that hundreds and hundreds of teens had already written in to ask for encouragement and guidance in their journey toward God. By the end of that first tour, more than a thousand had written in, telling us that they had begun a relationship with their Creator or that they wanted more information about how they could begin one!

I was overjoyed with the response of the young people, and as I flew home five weeks later, I knew that God had reached out to many of these young people just like He had reached out to me years earlier. It was so good to be a part of that.

Over the next year or so, I got follow-up e-mails from Africa. The teens were still writing in. Youth for Christ there was involving hundreds in Bible studies and the youth were growing in their faith. They held leadership camps, summer camps, and even a one-year missionary training school.

Johannes Kayimibi was a young man who had come to faith when we visited his high school and shared the Gospel. He subsequently attended the Youth for Christ leadership camps and the training school and became a missionary to his own people. I had not met him face to face when I was in Namibia that first time, but we would one day become good friends.

I found out from Jos Holtzhausen, director of Namibia Youth for Christ in those days, that Johannes was having a huge impact in the north of the country. He was working with teens in the schools, he was hosting Christian radio programs, and he was passing on the faith that had been passed on to him. Many young people were coming to trust God under the ministry of this young man.

A few years later, I returned to Namibia for another series of outreaches. It had been arranged for Johannes to accompany me on this trip, as well as another good friend of mine, a Canadian named Karl Janzen. It was great to go back to Africa with one of my best friends, and also fantastic to make a dear new friend in Johannes.

As we all sat having lunch one day, we talked about our lives and got to know each other. I met Johannes's lovely wife Pelgrina and their beautiful son Joshua. Realizing that we were in a heavy malaria region, I asked Johannes if he had ever contracted the disease.

"Oh no, I have not had malaria at all," he said. "I am so thankful. I have not had it this year at all!"

"You mean you have had malaria before?" I asked.

"Oh yes," Johannes replied matter-of-factly. "I've had it six or seven times." Karl and I just looked at each other. What a different world we were experiencing.

During part of this particular tour, we were required to have a military escort because we had to travel through a dangerous area called the Caprivi Strip, a place where Angolan rebels stole money, food, and supplies. AK-47 machine guns were all too plentiful in this area, and many people had already paid the rebels with their lives.

As we lined up with a few other cars, our military escort arrived. Five soldiers sat in the back of each truck, every man with his own fully automatic gun. A sixth man was responsible for the "big daddy" machine gun mounted in the back of the truck. The first military vehicle positioned itself at the front of our little convoy, the second truck brought up the rear.

Before we began our journey that morning, a soldier with a megaphone stood on the road and gave us instructions.

"If we come under attack today, pull your vehicle off the road and into the tall grass. Open your door and drop to the ground. Lie still in the tall grass. Do not attempt to make a run for it. If you try to run, that will be the last mistake you ever make." Johannes and I looked at each other with wide eyes. There were no actors here, no stuntmen, and no director shouting "action." This was real life.

After three hours of uneventful driving, the lead truck pulled over on the side of the road. The rest of the convoy followed.

"What's going on?" I asked nervously.

"Pee break," Johannes answered, an obvious look of relief on his face.

We climbed out of the truck and I made my way into a little grove of trees ten meters from the road. As I said farewell to the two cups of coffee I had enjoyed with breakfast, I looked back towards the truck and was somewhat shocked to see Johannes relieving himself right beside the truck, not far from the others, including women and children, in the convoy.

"Johnny!" I shouted, half-serious and half-teasing, "You need some manners! Come back here and do that in the bushes!"

Johannes replied in his usual gentle and understated way. "But Sam, you are standing in a landmine area."

I instantly froze. I could imagine the conversations that my wife would have with well-meaning friends back home: "Rita, I'm so sorry to hear that you lost your husband. Had he been ill?"

"No," would come Rita's tearful response. "Actually, he peed on a landmine in Africa." That scenario would never do! I mustered all the courage I had left and began the long, slow, gentle walk back to the vehicle, taking as few steps as humanly possible.

The rest of the trip was wonderful. As I spoke at the assemblies and told the students how God had changed and refocused my life, I would often ask Johannes to come up on stage and tell the story of how he had been invited to open his heart to Jesus.

"It was at an assembly just like this," he would tell the students. "God began to reach out to me, and I decided to follow Him. I knew that I needed forgiveness in my life, and the Lord poured that forgiveness over me. How could I not live in this new way?"

It was interesting to these young people that a black man from Namibia and a white man from Canada had so much obvious respect and love for each other. This really impacted the students and caused them to give our message a serious hearing. Again on this tour, many young people put their trust in Jesus and began a life-changing friendship with Him.

After thirty-five presentations for 20,000 young people, I returned home to Canada exhausted and happy. Not only did I have a Father in Heaven who had reached out to me in love, but I had a whole team of people back home and around the world who had experienced this same love and were committed to helping me share the story. By praying with us and for us, and by giving financially, they made these outreaches possible. Together, we were a great team.

It was about six months later that I heard from friends in Namibia that Johannes was in the hospital and deathly ill. A few days before he died, Johannes tested positive for HIV. He was dying from AIDS. It had been during his early high school days that Johannes became HIV-positive, though he never knew it until his last week of life.

In the years between coming to faith and dying in that hospital room in Namibia, Johannes touched thousands of lives. He loved people, and he served them with his whole heart. He passed his faith on to hundreds of others, and some of those people passed it on yet again.

Years later, I still think of that day in the minefield with Johannes. We all have our own minefields to walk through. Most of the time they don't involve actual physical bombs buried in the ground—often they are relational and emotional minefields, but they can be just as real and just as devastating. We all need help navigating the minefields of life. To think that we can do it all by ourselves is the height of arrogance. Johannes submitted his life to God, and God made his life count in mighty ways. I'm so thankful for my friend Johannes.

I miss him terribly.

CHAPTER TWELVE

A BIG FAMILY AND A VELVETEEN RABBIT
(Being Real Is More Important Than Being Beautiful)

With our young family entering the twenty-first century together, we were now up to four kids. Life was a blur of school band concerts, goodbyes at the airport, adventures in some remote or not-so-remote place on the globe, hellos at the airport, driving to baseball games, family dinners; you get the picture. Little Hannah had joined us and would forever be our youngest.

When I think of our family life, I think of a story called *The Velveteen Rabbit* by Margery Williams. It was first published in 1922, but will be just as relevant in 2022 and 2122.

It is the story of a little child's toy that struggles with its own significance. He sees the other toys, many of them mechanical and very modern. He decides to have a conversation with the skin horse, which has been there longer than anyone else.

> *"What is REAL?" asked the Rabbit one day, when they were lying side by side near the nursery fender, before Nana came to tidy the room. "Does it mean having things that buzz inside you and a stick-out handle?"*
>
> *"Real isn't how you are made," said the Skin Horse. "It's a thing that happens to you. When a child*

*loves you for a long, long time, not just to play with,
but REALLY loves you, then you become Real."*

"Does it hurt?" asked the Rabbit.

*"Sometimes," said the Skin Horse, for he was
always truthful. "When you are Real you don't mind
being hurt."*

*"Does it happen all at once, like being wound
up," he asked, "or bit by bit?"*

*"It doesn't happen all at once," said the Skin
Horse. "You become. It takes a long time. That's why
it doesn't happen often to people who break easily, or
have sharp edges, or who have to be carefully kept.
Generally, by the time you are Real, most of your
hair has been loved off, and your eyes drop out and
you get loose in the joints and very shabby. But these
things don't matter at all, because once you are Real
you can't be ugly, except to people who don't understand."*

*"I suppose you are real?" said the Rabbit. And
then he wished he had not said it, for he thought the
Skin Horse might be sensitive. But the Skin Horse
only smiled.**

I see family in this story—the honesty and pain of learning
to live with one another in all of our imperfections, yet knowing
that we still are, and always will be, loved. I see a beauty and
richness that can't be achieved with a hundred Beverly Hills
plastic surgeons or a thousand Hollywood fortunes.

In many ways, this speaks to the tragedy of marital and family breakdowns. As we raise a generation of young people who

---

* Williams, Margery. *The Velveteen Rabbit*. Doubleday & Company, Inc. Garden City, NY (1922).

do not see unconditional love modeled in their parents' relationship or experience unconditional love in their families, a deep-rooted fear becomes established. This fear causes us to reject others before we ourselves can be rejected, and this puts our present and future relationships at risk.

In order to bring the principles of *The Velveteen Rabbit* into our adult lives, I imagined a scenario where I was having a conversation with God. It went something like this...

"What is REAL?" I asked Jesus one day, as we sat by the big sharp rocks near the pier at White Rock beach. We both stared out at the vast Pacific Ocean, just as the tide began to come in. "Does it mean getting it all together and having people admire me for my skills and service in Your Kingdom?"

"Real isn't so much about what you do in public, it's who you are when no one's looking, it's how, and if, you allow Me to shape you," said the Lord. "It's a thing that happens to you. When you let Me love you for a long, long time, when you're not treating Me like a play thing, like a plastic doll, but you *really* let Me love you, then you become Real."

"Does it hurt?" I asked.

"Sometimes," He said, for He was always truthful. "When you are becoming real, you're sometimes willing to be hurt."

"Does it happen all at once, like a bolt of lightning," I asked, "or bit by bit?"

"It doesn't usually happen all at once," Jesus said. "Oh sure, there was Paul on that dusty road to Damascus. Sometimes My Father and I do it that way. But mostly it takes a long time. That's why it doesn't happen often to people who aren't desperate for Me, or to those who think they're better than others, or try to put themselves first. Generally, by the time you are Real, you spend more time thinking about Me and about others than you do thinking about yourself. Usually, by the time you're real, you're not one of the 'beautiful people' any more. But these things don't matter at all, because once you are Real you can't be ugly, except to people who don't understand."

"I suppose *you* are real?" I said to Jesus. And immediately I wished I had not said it—what a dumb thing for me to say. But He only smiled.

I have been privileged to meet more than my fair share of "real" people over the years. My litmus test for real people is very simple: if I feel smaller, weaker, and more discouraged from having spent time with a person, then they are probably not "real." If, however, I come away from a specific encounter with more hope, more courage, and more faith, I know that I have been in the presence of authenticity.

CHAPTER THIRTEEN

JOY IS A COMPLEX SUBJECT
(Jim Carrey and My Friend Ken Agree)

It seems that most people are carrying a secret shopping list for their lives. There are usually eight boxes that they want to tick off as they collect things necessary for an incredible life. With a few exceptions, the list looks like this:

- BOX ONE: Money—lots of it.
- BOX TWO: Popularity (adoration, if possible)
- BOX THREE: Great house.
- BOX FOUR: Great car.
- BOX FIVE: Great career.
- BOX SIX: Great body.
- BOX SEVEN: Great health.
- BOX EIGHT: Someone great to share it all with (or even better, someone else who brings all these things to the table!).

Because most of us never get all (or most) of the things on the list, we can continue the fantasy that the completed list would be the answer to all our prayers. Most of the advertising for lotteries supports this idea. They usually show ecstatically happy people whose lives really "began" when they won the big prize. The subtle underlying message is that the rest of us peons should patiently keep buying the lottery tickets until our big win comes and we join the ranks of those who are really living!

It's fascinating to me that of the ten people I write about in this book, not a single one could check off more than two or three of the boxes on the list above. In spite of that, joy is a major part of their lives and the impact they have had on others is immeasurable.

As I waited in a doctor's office recently, I found myself reading the quotes page in a Reader's Digest magazine. I came across a really honest and insightful thought from Jim Carrey, the very talented Canadian funnyman and actor. He said, "I think everybody should get rich and famous and do everything they ever dreamed of so they can see that it's not the answer."

Wow!

Jim Carrey has had it all: everything on that list. And yet he is honest enough to admit that it is not enough. Long-term joy is not found in having self-centered dreams come true.

"Okay," you say, "maybe joy is not found in having everything we want. But isn't joy mostly found when circumstances go our way and good things happen to us? I mean, can you really expect someone to be joyful when life is hard and when nasty things have happened or are happening to them?"

Enter my friend Ken.

Ken is a college professor at a west coast Canadian university. He is one of the most joyful people that I know, but he has not experienced an easy life. In spite of that, his life is full and rich.

When he was still a very young man, Ken married his best friend and together they began to build their lives. It only got better when their son Matthew was born on March 12, 1977. Matthew's name meant, "Gift from God," and he certainly was that in Ken's life. A wonderful daughter named Tamara followed a few years later. With his professional and family life blossoming, Ken had the world by the tail.

In the midst of the happiness and busyness of life, Ken's wife went on a trip to have a break. What she didn't tell Ken was that she was going on that trip with another man. When Ken found out, he was devastated, but he was also quick to try and put the pieces back together. As fast as he could glue and re-glue the broken pieces, they were smashed and then smashed again. Like all the king's men in the children's story, Ken was not able to put the pieces back together again.

As a single father, he worked very hard to provide and care for his young family. After more than a few years, a wonderful woman named Gabriela came into his life. She had three children of her own, and together they began to re-build. This new blended family slowly worked through the beauty and the complexity of making a life in concert with one another. With his professional and family life blossoming, Ken again had the world by the tail.

Life was happy and full of good things, until Ken developed health problems. He met with his doctor, who ran some tests. Then he ran a few more tests. Now, a week and a half later, Ken sat on a hard, wooden chair hearing the hard, unvarnished truth: "Ken, you have cancer. We need to operate."

During the surgery, the doctors removed thirty percent of Ken's colon. They tested his lymph nodes. It had been a rough ride, but the tests came back and he was clear of cancer.

It was a year or so later when Ken found himself back in his doctor's office. The oncologist was scanning the test results, wondering how he should break the news. He decided to just lay it out there. "Ken, there is a spot on your lung, and your liver is also showing a cancerous growth. I have to be honest with you, the odds are not good here."

What goes through one's mind at that point? Is it a feeling of complete and utter loss? Seething anger? Absolute despair?

Fortunately, this was not Ken's first scuffle in life. Word to the wise: don't ever let his huge grin and gentle demeanour fool you—Ken is a fighter. He was then and he is now. Tests, hospitalization, surgery on his lung, more tests, surgery on his liver, waiting, more tests, more waiting. Was he beat down? If he was, he didn't show it. Round after round, Ken took a pounding in the ring of life. It had to have taken a toll.

Finally, some great news: he was once again clear of cancer. It was time to stop fighting. It was time to rest, to regain his strength, to dream new dreams. For a guy that had been through so much, Ken had the world by the tail once again.

During all these years, Ken's precious "gift from God," Matthew, had become a man in his own right. He had finished his college degree, gotten married, and was following his dream to become a music minister at a church in the southern United States. And oh yes, he and his young bride were expecting a little gift of their own!

Ken was overjoyed as he watched his son's life unfold. What a gift Matthew had become to everyone around him. The thought of Matthew moving so far away was hard for Ken, but he was still the first one to volunteer to drive the U-haul down to Texas. Matthew and his wife Sarah would drive alongside in their car and join Ken in their two-vehicle convoy. It would be a real father-son-and-daughter-in-law bonding time.

As was expected, the three of them had a brilliant time driving all the way from Vancouver, Canada to San Antonio, Texas. They moved the furniture into Matthew and Sarah's little rental house, working hard to get things organized before Ken flew back a few days later.

"I love you, Dad," Matthew said as Ken left. "Thank you so much for everything you've done."

"I love you too, son," Ken replied, "I'll see you soon." Ken knew in his heart that he would not see his son soon, but "soon" could be a relative term, couldn't it? As Ken got on the flight back home, he was thanking God for the time he had with the son that he was already missing.

Life back in Vancouver was wonderful: his wife Gabi, the rest of their kids, students at the college, and friends at church and in the neighbourhood. All of these were gifts from God.

After a few short months, there was a phone call from Texas.

It was their daughter-in-law Sarah. Matthew had been hospitalized with severe breathing problems. As a child, Matthew had been diagnosed with chronic granulomatous disease, a disorder in which immune cells do not function properly. For the past eighteen years, however, he had been symptom-free... until now.

There were more questions than answers at this point, but one thing was for sure: this was serious. Ken and his daughter Tamara jumped on the first plane to Texas while Gabi made the tough choice to stay at home—their first grandchild was to be born at any moment in Vancouver.

Ken quietly walked into Matthew's hospital room, almost tiptoeing. He hadn't expected to see his son again so soon.

"Hello, Matthew," Ken whispered, too softly to be heard. The tears streamed down his face. His son's body lay there in front of him. How could he ever make sense of the fact that Matthew was gone?

Did Ken scream out and curse God for stealing his son? I might have been tempted to, but not Ken. Ken spoke to God and said, "Thank You."

"Thank You for the twenty-eight years that You gave me with Matthew," he prayed. "Thank You for a second chance at marriage with Gabi. Thank You for giving me life before, during and after cancer. My heart is broken in a million pieces. I feel as though I will never have joy again. But in this moment, in spite of where I find myself, I want to say thank You, God."

I want to say thank You, God.

Could it really be as uncomplicated as that? Is it simply a matter of choosing to be thankful for the time we have had with someone instead of cursing the time we have lost? Is it as straightforward as going over and over the things we love about someone instead of rehearsing the things that have disappointed or wounded us?

It is true that Ken's son Matthew is gone, and nothing can change that. But it is also true that Matthew's daughter Makenna was born a few months after her daddy passed on. How is it that our lives can be such a powerful juxtaposition of pain and joy? Will we allow the intensity and the colors of heartache and delight to produce a masterpiece beyond anything that would have been possible without them?

It is a gift that we experience life one moment at a time without knowing what the future will hold. For if we had the challenges and heartaches of a lifetime piled on our shoulders all at one time, who could withstand it? If the sorrows and joys come one or two at a time, though, maybe we can choose how we will see them. Maybe we can respond and not just react. Maybe there is a better way than the way that we've always done it.

Yesterday afternoon, my wife Rita and I attended a funeral. It was for Ken's mom, and there were hundreds of people there. Helen was eighty-five when she passed; she had led a fantastic life. We were sitting about five rows back, but we could see Ken in the front with the rest of his family. In the midst of missing his Mom and mourning her death, his arms were lifted high as he sang with a thankful heart, "It is well, it is well with my soul."

"*Life's not about waiting for the storms to pass... it's about learning to dance in the rain.*"

\- VIVIAN GREENE

CHAPTER FOURTEEN

MID-COURSE CORRECTIONS
(Where Do We Go From Here?)

We all get a little off-track sometimes. In his book *Mid-Course Correction*, Ray Anderson outlines what NASA scientists have discovered: that without mid-course corrections, their spacecrafts would be off course more than 90% of the time. Not only that, but without making these corrections, they would be on a path they never intended to travel, racing toward a destination they don't want to reach.[*]

Unfortunately, this misdirection affects many marriages and families as they too journey along a path they never intended to travel, towards a destination they don't want to reach. Without a change of heart and a change of direction, many of these marriages and families are heading for break-up, or, at the very least, cold and painful dysfunctionality.

Imagine the scene at Cape Canaveral in Florida: mission control radios the astronauts and tells them that they are heading off-course. They need to change their heading and adjust their trajectory. Would the astronauts say, "Are you kidding me? Get off my back! If you don't like my driving, get a new astronaut!"

---

[*] Anderson, Ray. *Mid-Course Correction: Toward a Sustainable Enterprise: The Interface Model*. Peregrinzilla Press (1999).

Of course not. The astronaut would probably say, "We are adjusting our course for the new heading. That looks good, Control. Thank you."

Like a man who doesn't want to ask for directions and look dumb, many guys push on with attitudes and actions in their family that are clearly not helpful. Even if those around point out that they are heading off-course, the temptation is to ignore the warning voices or even smash the blinking red engine light on the dashboard. I know this is true because I have been one of those men.

For me, one of my great challenges has been a lifelong struggle with anger. I grew up with a very angry person in my life (not my dad or mom). This person threw his weight around and was verbally and physically abusive on a regular basis. While I suffered under the wrath of this person, it also appeared to me that this person mostly got what he wanted. People did what he wanted, when he wanted it.

While convincing myself that I was nothing like this "role model," I subconsciously began to utilize a toned-down version of those same manipulative techniques. I convinced myself that it was in the other person's best interests and that I shouldn't have to put up with their "stuff." This resulted in me yelling at the kids and Rita, and losing my cool on countless occasions. While I never crossed the line and became physically abusive, my anger often became a bigger issue than whatever the original problem was that we were dealing with.

Like an alcoholic, I denied that I had a problem for years. It was always someone else's fault that I lost my cool. "He should know better," or "Did you see what that driver in front of me did?" became my favourite tactics for denying my own responsibility.

The funny thing is, people outside of my immediate family were often shocked if I confessed that I struggled with anger.

"Wow, Sam, not you," they would say. "You're the last person I would think of as being angry." For some reason, I was able to control my temper when I was out and about, but at home it was a different story.

The Bible has a lot to say about how we should interact with one another. Look at 1 Peter 3:15—"*Always be prepared to give an answer to everyone who asks you to give the reason for the hope that you have. But do this with gentleness and respect.*"

If we are supposed to treat people with gentleness and respect, must that not also include our spouse, our parents, our children, and our in-laws? The ideas contained in 1 Peter 3:15 have become a very important theme for me, and I have modified it slightly for use at home: "Always be prepared to give a reason for the issue that you need to discuss with your wife or children. But do this with gentleness and respect, honouring them as the incredible gifts from God that they are."

It seems that I need to make daily, even hourly, mid-course corrections. It's a bit humbling, but at least I spend a little less time going down roads that I don't want to travel towards destinations that I don't want to reach.

I once heard a speaker somewhere say, "Fast forward your DVD and see if you like how it ends." He explained that we should examine anything important to us: our relationships, our finances, anything. Think of that particular issue or relationship as a movie. Now, "fast forward" it. If you keep doing what you have been doing, how is that situation likely to play out? Do you feel good about how that movie will end? If not, make the changes necessary to transform the plot and the remainder of the scenes.

Why is it that we spend so much time and energy thinking, worrying, and obsessing about things that we cannot change and yet we avoid making decisions and taking action in areas where we have the power to make a real difference? If we want to experience real change in our lives, we should remember this quote from an anonymous philosopher: "To get what we've never had, we must do what we've never done."

Making mid-course corrections and "fast-forwarding" are habits that I want to develop. We have been given the power to change the plot. Will we dare to do it?

CHAPTER FIFTEEN

FREEDOM IN A RWANDAN PRISON
(What Does Freedom Really Mean?)

As we drove toward the old prison, government documents in hand, we wondered aloud what the next few hours would hold. We were in Kigali, Rwanda, a country famous for death. More precisely, we were in a country known for the death of a million people in a one hundred day stretch in 1994. Not wiped out in one shot by an atomic bomb or in large groups during organized military campaigns, but mostly killed one man, one woman, and one child at a time. They were killed not by guns—the ammunition would have been too expensive. Instead, it was human hands wrapped tightly around the handle of a waving machete, repeated a million times.

The old imposing walls of the prison met us like a giant tombstone, out of place amongst the lush green flora all around us. We drove to the far end of the prison, and I was taken aback to see men walking like zombies and covered in grey ash working around a fifteen-foot cast iron pot. It had the feel of a World War II newsreel—the ones that the Allied Forces had filmed, showing prisoners so weak that they would never tell their stories except in the newsreel itself.

We entered through a side gate and went through the customary bureaucracy of any prison, anywhere in the world. As we carried our sound equipment through this gate and that gate, prisoners came alongside and helped carry the load. At first, I was concerned that our gear would be stolen, then quickly decided that was not the worst thing that could happen to us. Strangely, I started to relax.

As we got closer to the big room being used as an auditorium, we could hear singing. The vibrant, rich music started to envelope us as the final door was opened. A choir was just finishing up and we were ushered onto the stage to set up our gear and begin.

As we set to work, a tall, well-dressed man spoke to a crowd of eight hundred inmates wearing pink coveralls, standard issue for prisoners in Rwanda. I found out that this M.C. normally spoke or translated at special Christian outreaches when they were held at the prison.

A local pastor or perhaps a Christian businessman? I thought to myself. *There is something special about him. I would really like to meet that man.*

The thing that most impressed me was not his well-tailored clothes, his commanding presence, or his rich baritone voice. This man spoke into that sea of humanity with a profound dignity that originated in him, but poured over them.

I spent the next hour singing, challenging, and reaching out to those prisoners. They were attentive and responsive, even though I had to speak through the interpreter. It was amusing to hear two waves of laughter when anything funny was said. It gave me a clear gauge of how many spoke English and how many did not. I spoke about hope and freedom—that the forgiveness and friendship of God offered us the opportunity to be free, no matter what our circumstances were.

"If your first concern is to look after yourself, you'll never find yourself. But if you forget about yourself and look to me, you'll find both yourself and me," Jesus says in Matthew 10:39 (MSG). I wanted them to take

hold of the message that God was offering freedom and life, if only we would let go of ourselves and take hold of Him.

Many of the prisoners responded, holding their hands up to God and saying, "Forgive me. Help me to make a new start. Change my life!" As I led the men in prayer, the tall well-dressed man continued to translate for me, his hand on the shoulder of the prisoner kneeling closest to him. After we prayed over the prisoners individually, the guards came and cleared the room. I was left there with my translator and finally had a chance to speak with him directly.

"Thank you so much for the ministry that you have with these men," I said. "I understand that you take time from your schedule to come and make a difference in these men's lives whenever there is a Christian outreach or special event."

"It was such a pleasure to serve with you," was his humble response.

"I want you to know how important your work here is," I said. "I can come here maybe once every two years, but you come regularly to help and to encourage these men. Do you come once a month, or maybe every two weeks?"

"Perhaps you do not understand," he replied. "I am a prisoner here."

"Are you serious?" I asked, too surprised to be polite. "How long have you been in jail here?"

"Since 1996," he answered calmly, with no hint of bitterness.

"When will you be released?" I asked.

"I don't know when I might be released, Sam," he said, stunning me. "I don't really care, because I'm free. I am free if I stay in this prison and I am free if I am released, so it doesn't matter. God has made me free."

He shook my hand once again and then left with the guard who had silently joined us during our conversation.

I stood alone, wondering how a man who was now being escorted to his cell had more freedom and joy in his life than I did. One day, I hope to be as free as Prisoner #96208.

CHAPTER SIXTEEN

LOOKING BACK, LOOKING FORWARD
(Our Family Continues By Faith)

Twenty-five years ago, God first asked me to step out of my comfort zone and give up control of my life. Just like the Carrie Underwood song *Jesus, Take the Wheel*, God asked me if I would be willing to move over and ride shotgun with Him through the adventures that He had planned for us. My comfort zone has definitely grown over the years, encompassing many cities and countries around the world. What I didn't expect was that my comfort zone was about to be tested from within the boundaries of my own home.

It all began with a drive to our local hospital, Surrey Memorial, to see an old work friend named Terry Ducommun. Terry had been struggling with cancer for a few years, but that was only a small piece of the whole story.

Terry and his first wife, Julie, had married many years before. Unable to have children of their own, they adopted a little girl and then three years later, a little boy.

By the time their adopted son Tanner was eighteen months old, Julie was diagnosed with breast cancer. A few weeks after his third birthday, Tanner lost the only mom he had ever known.

Terry did his very best to raise his two children, and after five or six years, he fell in love again. As he was about to ask his new love to marry him, he received devastating news: he had a very aggressive form of skin cancer. Terry went ahead with his proposal, and while his fiancé said yes to marriage, she also explained that she felt unable to care for his children should he not survive.

They had now been married for eighteen months, and health-wise things were not looking good. After my visit with Terry in the hospital, I came home and told Rita about our time together and about the situation he was facing. Our two oldest girls, who were nineteen and seventeen at the time, were together in one of the bedrooms, and overheard our conversation.

"You know," Dana quietly said to Tanaya, "those kids are going to come and live with us."

At the very same moment, unaware of the conversation our two children were having, Rita looked me in the eye and said, "Are you thinking what I'm thinking?"

I was not ready to deal with this potential challenge to my comfort zone and I was also getting ready to leave on another African adventure in less than twenty-four hours, so I suggested we pray during the month that I would be away.

Was it really possible that God was asking Rita and me to "enlarge our tent" and invite these two children to join our four biological children? While over in Namibia, I reflected on the fact that during concerts and preaching engagements, I had poured my faith and life one or two hours at a time into thousands and thousands of people that I didn't know. Now, were we to pour thousands and thousands of hours into one or two people in our own home—people who were every bit as much strangers to us?

After I returned from Africa, Rita and I met with Terry and his wife and shared our willingness to open our home to Tanner and his older sister Jenna should they need us. Terry was overjoyed and said that a huge burden had been lifted off his back. The two children moved in with us about a month before their dad passed on. Unfortunately, Jenna found the concept of family too difficult to re-adapt to and chose a more independent life-style. In spite of that, we have tried to provide direction and support to her in what has proven to be a very difficult situation. Two years have quickly passed since Terry's death. Tanner has changed from a small boy into a tall young man. It has been a poignant and unprecedented journey for our entire family. We have found it vital to understand that opening one's home to people in need is every bit as much a step of faith as going to the other side of the planet as a missionary or aid worker.

In fact, to serve anyone in love takes a lot of faith. Think about the people in your own life. It takes faith to love your spouse and to serve him or her when you're not "feelin' it." It takes faith to love and care for your child when they are going through a difficult or rebellious stage. It takes faith and love to serve an aging parent who is struggling with their health. It takes faith and love to pour into others when you don't see an immediate return on your investment.

C.S. Lewis once said, "Relying on God has to begin all over again every day as if nothing had yet been done." Faith has to be new every morning. Hope has to be new every morning. Love has to be new every morning. We can't live on last week's, or last month's, supply.

What fresh step of faith is waiting for you today?

CHAPTER SEVENTEEN

FROM DEATH ROW TO SIMCHA
(Simcha: Life and Joy in the Fullest Sense)

I am crazy enough to believe that depression, anxiety, and a life drained of color and hope should not be our normal, on-going experience. Yes, we are all familiar with most, or maybe all, of these negative emotions. Yet these ten remarkable people have convinced me that there can be much more in this life. Once again, I discovered "simcha" (noun of Hebrew origin: "life and joy in the fullest sense") in the most unlikely place: death row.

We sometimes hear about people on death row. They are mostly in faraway places. They are almost always people we have never met. I had certainly never met a death row inmate, until I was on a tour on the beautiful island nation of Mauritius, just off the east coast of Madagascar.

Soon after arriving on Mauritius, I was introduced to the man who would translate for me at several of the events, Ponsamy (Sam) Poongavanon.

Sam Poongavanon taught me some things that no one else ever has. As he shared his story with me a few months ago, it made me think very earnestly about an issue that affects you and I every day. There are times when you may feel that you have wasted parts of your life because of choices you have made or choices others have made on your behalf.

But the real question should be: What choices are you making with the time that you have left? This is the core of Ponsamy (Sam) Poongavanon's story.

In 1985, Sam was a young man of twenty-eight, madly in love. Unfortunately, the love of his life was also involved with another man. For some reason, his girlfriend had arranged for the three of them to meet together. Several days later, there they were. Sam was in the passenger side of the front seat beside the "other man." His girlfriend was in the back.

Suddenly, a shot rang out and the man behind the steering wheel slumped over, dead. In shock, Sam looked back to see his girlfriend holding a gun. He immediately told her to run; he would stay and take the heat for it. The police arrived and arrested Sam. He told the police that he had been alone with the man. Evidence and DNA testing showed that someone else had been in the back seat of the car, but the police had a confession and, besides, there were other crimes to solve.

As Sam waited for his court case, he longed to see the love of his life, the woman whom he had given everything up for. She did not come to see him in those two years that he waited to be judged. She did send word, however, that she had fallen in love with someone else and was moving out of the country. How convenient. Could his life get any worse?

The agony of his choice haunted Sam every hour of every day. How could he have been so stupid as to give up his freedom and his life to protect someone who had quickly moved on to other lovers and who seemed to have no problem allowing him to suffer, and perhaps even die, in her place?

Two years later, in 1987, Sam had his day in court. He will never forget the sound of the judge's voice on that Saturday in March. Sam was thirty years old when he was sentenced to hang by the neck until he was dead.

Rage overwhelmed his every waking moment. His anger had three well-defined targets: the woman who had started this cycle of events, the policemen who had beat him mercilessly in prison, and the judge who had sentenced him to die for a crime he did not commit.

On top of everything else, Sam, like all death row inmates in Mauritius, was kept in solitary confinement. He could see daylight for only thirty minutes in the morning and thirty minutes in the evening. The rest of the time, it was fluorescent lights or total darkness. He spent the first five years of his sentence in solitary confinement, waiting to die. He had plenty of time to consider his situation and the people who had put him there.

Over the years, he began to search for some kind of peace because living in that hell seemed much worse than dying by the rope could ever be. The son of a Hindu priest, Sam searched the Hindu scriptures. He also read the Koran from cover to cover. Meanwhile, his lawyer made an appeal for the court to spare Sam's life. The judge responded by setting Sam's execution date for the following Tuesday—not exactly the response he was hoping for.

Someone in the prison gave Sam a book called *The Story of Sadhu Sundar Singh*. Singh was also of Indian decent but came from a Sikh background and had become a follower of Jesus. Sam told himself, "I will never read this book." But, strangely enough, he woke up early the next morning with a hunger to investigate this man's story. Over the next few hours, Sam consumed the book from cover to cover.

The next day, he asked the guards if they would get him a Bible. Because he was a Hindu, it was illegal for them to give it to him. He went on a hunger strike in an attempt to get a Bible for himself. Two of the guards began to argue with each other about whether he should get a Bible or not.

"Just give it to him," one of the guards finally said. "He's going to hang in a few days anyway!"

Having received a Bible, Sam read it voraciously. Meanwhile, his lawyer managed to get a brief stay of execution while he appealed to the Privy Council in London, England.

As Sam read the Bible, he came across Matthew 18:35, where Jesus said that unless we forgive others from the heart, God will not forgive us. This shook him to the core. He felt that it was impossible for him to forgive. What hope did he have?

Shaken, he cried out to God with his whole heart. "You have told me that I must forgive, but I don't see how I can possibly do it," he prayed. "And yet You have commanded it, and if You have commanded it, it must be possible somehow. God, do in me what I cannot do in myself. Give me Your Spirit of forgiveness." He began to pray for the judge, the policeman, and the woman who had committed the murder. He realized that whether he was in or out of prison, he would be a prisoner until his unforgiveness was dealt with in his heart.

Sam read Isaiah 55:8-9, where God said,

> "For my thoughts are not your thoughts, neither are your ways my ways," declares the LORD. "As the heavens are higher than the earth, so are my ways higher than your ways and my thoughts than your thoughts."

Sam cried out for God's thoughts and God's ways. Slowly at first, and then with great power, Sam began to experience God's uncompromising and unmistakable freedom in his own life.

Even though he was still in the Mauritian prison, he was free from the emotional and spiritual prisons that threaten all of us. He was free from the prison of hopelessness, and it did not go unnoticed. He became the talk of the prison, and soon his story was going out across all of Mauritius.

On April 29, 1992, Sam's death sentence was rescinded in what the Mauritian legal system called a "commutation of sentence."

In place of the death sentence, Sam was left with a twenty-year prison term (five years of solitary confinement served and fifteen years of jail time to go). Sam made the most of this time, studying in prison and trying to make a difference in the lives of those around him. He wrote his autobiography and published it from the jail. He was invited to share his story with other prisoners. The media picked up his story, broadcasting it on radio, television, and in newspapers.

At exactly 7:00 a.m. on Tuesday, March 27, 2007, Sam stepped out into physical freedom for the first time in more than twenty years. Reporters from the local media covered the story that had caught the attention of the country—the falsely accused Hindu death row inmate who claimed to have met Jesus Christ in the depths of his hopelessness.

During his darkest hours in solitary confinement, Sam had challenged Jesus by saying, "If You are really alive, if You have done all these amazing things, do a miracle in my life, and I will tell Your story everywhere I go."

Would you and I dare to cry out for a miracle on God's terms, or is giving up our control too high a price to pay?

Sam Poongavanon discovered life after death row. He experienced spring in the middle of winter.

Now it's our turn.

CHAPTER EIGHTEEN

FINDING SPRING ON THE INSIDE
(Hope for the Journey)

Afew years ago, my friends Peter and Elsje Hannah gave me a book called *Children's Letters to God*. As one looks through this collection of notes written by open and honest little hearts, it causes the reader to let down his guard and enter into the wonder and mystery and beauty of life. Some of these "letters to God" are very funny. A young man named Sam says, "Dear God, I want to be just like my Daddy when I get big, but not with so much hair all over!" Nan says, "Dear God, I bet it is very hard for You to love all of everybody in the whole world. There are only four people in our family and I can never do it!"[*]

Some of the letters are quite touching. Eugene writes, "Dear God, I didn't think that orange went with purple until I saw the sunset you made on Tuesday. That was cool." A little girl named Nora penned her note to God saying, "I don't ever feel alone since I heard about You." Then there is Frank who writes, "Dear God, I'M DOING THE BEST I CAN!"

As I read through the book, I realized that there were some letters I might have written myself, had I dared to be that honest. What a poignant moment when I came across the letter from a boy named Mark. Of all the notes in the book, this letter

---

[*] Hample, Stuart and Eric Marshall. *Children's Letters to God*. Workman Publishing Company (1991).

resonated within me the loudest. It simply says: "Dear God, I keep waiting for spring but it never come yet. Don't forget."

As I type these words, it is spring in Vancouver, Canada. For the past few years, I have been on some other continent at this time of year, so I have missed what goes on here in April, May, and June.

Life is breaking out in great gaudy gobs all around me. Muddy ground is turning into beautiful green meadows. Shrunken shrubs are exploding with color and light. Once-silent forests are erupting with song both day and night: the rat-a-tat-tat of woodpeckers, the howl of the coyotes. I hear friends and relatives singing to each other from one nest to another. The beauty is breathtaking! There is even pink "snow" that falls from the blossoming trees.

How heartbreaking it would be to have spring all around us, but the dead of winter in our hearts. Spring comes to this earth every single year, but how long has it been since spring came to you?

We all desperately need spring. Too many of us experience an inner life like that of frozen Narnia where it was "always winter and never Christmas." Yes, there are things that break our hearts, but we were never designed to live that way, year after year after year.

Will you experience spring on a regular basis, or will you be dead and cold inside? It all depends on what shopping mall you go to.

Shopping mall? Say what?! Let me explain.

The "If Only" Shopping Super Centre is the first shopping mall that greets us. If we walk through this mall, we will see stores called "If Only I Were Married" and "If Only I Wasn't Married," among others. There are actually thousands of stores in this mall, and their names all begin with "If Only." If only my finances weren't a disaster. If only my parents never divorced. If only my kids would smarten up. The list goes on and on. Go ahead, think of a few of the stores in your "If Only" shopping mall. Life would be great "If Only..."

Now stop. You have a choice to make. What percentage of the rest of your life do you want to spend in that "If Only" mall? Remember, being there doesn't change a thing. It is really a holding tank that is devoid of life. Spring will never be found in that place.

"The Mall of Problems" is the next shopping center to check out. This one is actually a strip mall, meaning you can sit in your car in the parking lot and view all the stores from there, each one named after a major problem in your life. One store is called "My Health Problems." The next store is "My Relationship Problems." There are even specialty "niche" stores. Instead of Hugo Boss, there is "My Stupid Boss." Instead of Old Navy there is "Old Football Injury." And on and on it goes.

Some people are trading away their lives, a day at a time, as they sit and live in their problems. Days become weeks, weeks become months, and months become years. You know the type. You only ask them "How are you doing?" once because if they get the chance, they'll pull you into their "car" and spend the next forty minutes pointing out all their personal favourites in their strip mall of problems.

I am not saying that we should avoid, or never discuss our problems. If there is something that can be done to deal with a problem, than we should deal with it. But in my experience, going over and over problems in our minds, or verbally with others who can't really help, is about as useful as shopping in the mall of "If Only." If you choose to hang out in the strip mall of problems, you can be guaranteed that spring will not come to you.

Whenever I have experienced spring in my life, it has always come the same way. It comes to me when I turn my back on "If Only" living and walk away from the strip mall of my problems.

But it is not enough just to walk away from things—we must walk toward something, or, more specifically, toward someone. If we dare to take the center of who we are, the most fragile, precious part of ourselves and send it on ahead to our Creator, we will experience spring. It is spelled out in Hosea 6:3 (NLT):

> *Oh, that we might know the Lord!*
> *Let us press on to know him.*
> *He will respond to us as surely as the arrival of dawn*
> *Or the coming of rains in early spring.*

If we "press on" to know God, He will respond to us. His response is as definite as the rains of early spring in Vancouver. His response *brings* life. His response *is* life.

As He responds to us, He begins to shape our hopes and dreams. What is important to Him becomes important to us. In Acts 13:36, it says that, "*[King David] served God's purpose in his own generation.*" Maybe our dreams are too small! This short portion of Scripture indicates that it is possible for human beings to partner with the Creator of the universe to help make God's dreams come true.

That sounds like spring to me. That sounds like beautiful green meadows, explosions of color and light, eruptions of song. That sounds like friends and relatives and even strangers singing to each other from their homes, their cities, and their countries. The beauty is breathtaking!

The ten people you've never met have sung this song to me and now I want to sing it to you. Will you dare to pick up the tune and sing, with reckless abandon, at the top of your lungs?

You may think that there are too many things standing between you and the life that you were born to live, but really there is only one thing in your way—one single thing. It is not your marital status, your financial status, or any other status. It is not your education, your family, or your job. It is not your past, your present, or your future. The only thing that has the potential to stop you in your tracks is fear.

It is no coincidence that author Lloyd Ogilvie has discovered the most frequent instruction in the Bible is "Do not be afraid!" In fact, some form of "fear not" appears 366 times in Scripture. God made it so that we would have one "fear not" verse for every day of the year—even during leap years. Over and over again, God chooses to emphasize this idea of overcoming fear. The way He intuitively understands us, our weaknesses, and our fears, one might almost believe that He made us!

I recently met with a friend of mine who seems to have given up on his marriage. He told me his challenges and said that he just couldn't take it any more. Though he didn't use these exact words, the message, "If only she would change," came across loud and clear. So, as a friend, I spent some time with him in the "If Only" Shopping Super Centre. Then he laid out some of the other problems he was facing—financial problems, relationship problems. Again, as a friend, I was willing to be with him in the "The Mall of Problems" for a time.

Finally, after an hour and a half, I asked him what his favourite movie was. *Lord of the Rings*, he replied.

"What makes it your favourite?" I asked.

"Well", he said, "there's great action, great conflict, great challenges, and great sacrifice for a greater goal."

I let his words sink in and then asked another question: "Why is it that we all want action, adventure, and great challenges in the movies we watch, but when it happens for real in our lives, we think that God has abandoned us? You are in the middle of your own *Lord of the Rings* and this is your time to serve your wife, to risk everything to save your family, or die trying."

In the second installment of the *Lord of the Rings* trilogy, there is an amazing dialogue between Frodo and Sam:

> Sam: "It's like in the great stories, Mr. Frodo, the ones that really mattered. Full of darkness and danger they were, and sometimes you didn't want to know the end because how could the end be happy? Those were the stories that stayed with you, that meant something even if you were too small to understand why. But I think, Mr. Frodo, I do understand. I know now folk in those stories had lots of chances of turning back, only they didn't. They kept going because they were holding onto something.
>
> Frodo: "What are we holding onto, Sam?"
>
> Sam: "That there's some good in the world, Mr. Frodo, and it's worth fighting for."

Right at this moment, you need to know that your story matters. It might be full of darkness and danger. You certainly have the chance to turn back if you should choose to. But here is the central question: Whatever battle you are fighting in life, are you willing to risk everything to see it through or die trying?

You might be afraid to continue in the battle, but if you want spring bad enough, you'll have to walk right over your fear. The plain truth is that spring and fear are incompatible with each another.

It was a young boy named Mark who wrote the letter to God that inspired this chapter. I share his heartfelt note once again.

"Dear God, I keep waiting for spring but it never come yet. Don't forget."

If those words resonate in your heart like they did in mine, I hope you will dare to begin a journey that no one else can take for you. I cannot give you a map or a GPS locator to help you find the way, but I can share with you the words that act as guideposts for me.

Combining Hosea 6:3 and Acts 13:36 gives me a simple sentence that helps me every day—"Oh, that we might know the Lord and serve God's purpose in our own generation."

This is spring. This is life. This is the beautiful green meadow.

CHAPTER NINETEEN

WHAT DO THE TEN PEOPLE HAVE IN COMMON?

L et's take a moment to review the ten wonderful real people you've never met:

1. Pastor Kandume (the rich man without money).
2. Valencia (the one-legged dancer).
3. The Peruvian shoeshine boy.
4. The old lady in Peru (mixing cement).
5. The blind Burmese children.
6. Baby Bryce (Twenty minutes to say I love you).
7. Johannes Kayimbi (landmine area).
8. Ken Pudlas (finding real joy on the dark days).
9. Free man in the Rwandan prison (Convict #96208).
10. Ponsamy (Sam) Poongavanon (death row to amazing life).

These people have a lot in common, but they also have a number of differences, including:

- Nationality—they come from seven different countries on four different continents.
- Age—some are young, some are middle-aged, and some are old.

- Gender—some are men and some are women.
- Economic status—some are middle class, while others are very poor by world standards.

Putting aside the Peruvian shoeshine boy, whom I didn't know well, and baby Bryce, who died as an infant, I see that the others have faced challenges that would have destroyed lesser souls. Consider what they have in common:

- They are all courageous people.
- They are all forgiving people.
- They all exude a sense of humility.
- They all live in their present, not their past.
- None of them are clogged by fear.
- They are all thankful people.
- They all want to make a difference in other people's lives.
- They all set an example that is worth following.

As I think about what they have in common, the greatest "what" is actually not a "what" at all, but a "who." Every single one of these people have let down their guard and made a conscious decision to trust God by putting their faith in Jesus. Maybe that sounds strange, crazy, radical, or weird to you, but it's the truth. If we want real change in our lives, we need to be willing to make mid-course corrections. As I quoted earlier in the book, *"To get what we've never had, we must do what we've never done."*

But what must we do?

Many people think that getting right with God means cleaning ourselves up and following the rules so that we will be good enough for Him. Sorry, but I can't sign up for that program. How will I know if I am ever good enough? In fact, I don't think I can be good enough!

I'm so glad that the Bible makes it clear that it is *God* who makes the changes in us, not we in ourselves. We only need to give him the freedom and the invitation to do it. In Romans 12:1, it says that, *"Embracing what God does for you is the best thing you can do for Him"* (MSG). He changes everything if we come to Him with sincere hearts and put our lives into His hands.

Jesus Christ is the common denominator among the ten people you've never met. You may not have the privilege of meeting any of these ten wonderful people, but you still can have the privilege of meeting Jesus Christ.

Some people might say that Jesus was a great moral teacher, but nothing more than that. The famous British writer C.S. Lewis responds to this idea in his book *Mere Christianity*—

> *I am trying here to prevent anyone saying the really foolish thing that people often say about Him: 'I'm ready to accept Jesus as a great moral teacher, but I don't accept his claim to be God.' That is the one thing we must not say. A man who was merely a man and said the sort of things Jesus said would not be a good moral teacher. He would either be a lunatic-on a level with the man who says he is a poached egg— or else he would be the Devil of Hell. You must make your choice.*
>
> *Either this man was, and is, the Son of God: or else a madman or something worse. You can shut Him up for a fool, you can spit at Him and kill Him as a demon; or you can fall at His feet and call Him Lord and God. But let us not come with any patron-*

izing nonsense about His being a great moral teacher. He has not left that open to us. He did not intend to.

The most important question is "What do we do with Jesus?" I suppose we can ignore Him, we can hate Him, or we can turn to Him with our whole heart and experience His life.

This is simpler than we think, as we read in Romans 12:1-2 (MSG):

> *So here's what I want you to do, God helping you: Take your everyday, ordinary life—your sleeping, eating, going-to-work, and walking-around life— and place it before God as an offering. Embracing what God does for you is the best thing you can do for him. Don't become so well-adjusted to your culture that you fit into it without even thinking. Instead, fix your attention on God. You'll be changed from the inside out. Readily recognize what he wants from you, and quickly respond to it. Unlike the culture around you, always dragging you down to its level of immaturity, God brings the best out of you, develops well-formed maturity in you.**

It's as simple as saying (praying) to God:

> *Hi God, This is _____. I realize how much I need You. Thank You for reaching out to me. Please forgive me for where I've screwed up and lived selfishly. Forgive me for wanting to do this all on my own. Help me to know You, to really know You. I need a new start.*

---

* Lewis, C.S. *Mere Christianity*. HarperOne (3rd Edition, 2001).

Thank You that You can forgive me of my failures and mistakes because Jesus paid for it all when He died on the cross. Thank You that You brought Him back to life after three days. I need that kind of life in my life! Help me to live unselfishly. Take my life and use in a way that pleases you. Amen."

That is not the end of the story, though—it's just the beginning. It's the first step in the journey of a lifetime. Each of our ten people that were old enough to make this decision made it in favour of Jesus. He became the change point for their lives. He became the change point for my life. And He can become the change point for your life, too.

EPILOGUE

It is impossible to experience true life in the "If Only" Shopping Super Centre or the "Problem" Strip Mall, but walking away from either of those places takes real courage.

It feels dangerous to even think about letting go of the things that hold us back from living, because we secretly use them to insulate ourselves from the potential of additional pain. Yes, we sometimes hold onto old pain to shield ourselves from the possibility of fresh, new pain. And though it is dangerous to let go of it, it is fatal to hold onto it.

Surprisingly, there is something we fear even more than letting go of our pain and garbage. We fear being empty-handed. Yet unless we allow ourselves to become empty-handed, we can never take hold of the good, life-giving things we so desperately need.

Here is a profound thought: There is nothing stopping you from really living except your own unwillingness to really live.

If a death row inmate in Africa, a poor crippled woman with one eye in South America, and a blind child who was cast off by her parents in Southeast Asia can find real life, I think you and I can, too.

If I was to sum up what I have learned from these ten people, it would be this: To really live, we must be willing to let go of, and then to take hold of. We must be willing to let go of guilt, bitterness, and fear itself. We must be willing to take hold of faith, forgiveness, and freedom. Three things to let go of. Three things to take hold of.

In Matthew 10:39, Jesus said, *"If you cling to your life, you will lose it; but if you give up your life for me, you will find it"* (NLT). In other words, he says, "Do you want real life? More life than you ever thought possible? Then give it away because of My love for you. Give it away because of your love for Me. Live like you were dying."

  Live like you were dying. Country singer Tim McGraw recorded a song by that title, and I love the lyrics in the chorus, which say—

> *I went skydiving.*
>
> *I went Rocky Mountain climbing.*
>
> *I went two point seven seconds on a bull named Fu Man Chu.*
>
> *And I loved deeper,*
>
> *And I spoke sweeter,*
>
> *And I gave forgiveness I'd been denyin',*
>
> *And he said some day I hope you get the chance*
>
> *To live like you were dyin'...* *

You and I have that chance today. Not yesterday. Not tomorrow. Today.

In fact, it starts right now.

---

* *Live Like You Were Dying,* by Tim Nichols and Craig Michael Wiseman. Warner-Tamerlane Publishing Corp. (2004)

ABOUT THE AUTHOR

Sam Rowland is a speaker, author, and musician. He has shared his story and his music with the tribal peoples of Namibia, Africa. The secret police came to every concert he did in Myanmar, Asia. His songs have stirred the hearts of people in the jungle hills of Jamaica, West Indies. He has opened his heart unashamedly to share his journey in great cities and little villages on the European continent. Concert tours have taken him from coast to coast in both the United States and in his "home and native land" of Canada.

By weaving together humour, music, and thought-provoking insights, Sam has impacted thousands of people on five continents. He has also recorded six CDs as well as a DVD called *Words & Music... Live from Europe*.

Sam, his wife Rita, and their four children live in Vancouver, British Columbia, Canada.

Requests for information should be addressed to:

Sam Rowland

c/o Youth Unlimited Phone: (604) 590-3759

#115-12975 84th Avenue Fax: (604) 590-6237

Surrey, BC V3W 1B3 E-mail: samrowland@telus.net

Canada   Website: www.samrowland.org